W9-CBH-564

THE CONSCIENCE
OF A LIBERAL

Senator Paul Wellstone

THE

CONSCIENCE

OF A

LIBERAL

Reclaiming the
Compassionate Agenda

RANDOM HOUSE

NEW YORK

Copyright © 2001 by Paul David Wellstone

All rights reserved under International and Pan-American Copyright Conventions.
Published in the United States by Random House, Inc., New York, and simultaneously
in Canada by Random House of Canada Limited, Toronto.

Grateful acknowledgment is made to The Washington Post Writer's Group
for permission to reprint an excerpt from a column by William Raspberry from
the March 8, 1999, edition of *The Washington Post*. Copyright © 1999 by
The Washington Post Writer's Group. Reprinted with permission.

Library of Congress Cataloging-in-Publication Data
Wellstone, Paul.
The conscience of a liberal: reclaiming
the compassionate agenda / Paul Wellstone.
p.   cm.
ISBN 0-679-46294-5
1. Wellstone, Paul David. 2. Legislators—United States—Biography.
3. United States. Congress. Senate—Biography. 4. Liberalism—United States. I. Title.
E840.8.W47 A3 2001   328.73'092—dc21
[B]   00-066493

Manufactured in the United States of America on acid-free paper
24689753
First Edition

Book design by J. K. Lambert

TO SHEILA

After thirty-seven years of marriage, I am not objective.
But I love loving and working with you.

TO MIKE EPSTEIN

You were my teacher. You made me a good senator.

TO RICK KAHN

Everyone should be blessed to have a friend like you.

TO MY CHILDREN, DAVID, MARCIA, AND MARK,
AND TO MY GRANDCHILDREN, CARI, KEITH, JOSHUA,
MATT, ACACIA, AND SIDNEY

I love you.

TO MY PARENTS, MINNIE AND LEON

I know you know—your son is a U.S. senator.
Don't worry—I'm a liberal!

CONTENTS

INTRODUCTION

There is one lesson I have learned that I hold above all others from my experience as a father, teacher, community organizer, and U.S. senator: We should never separate the lives we live from the words we speak. To me, the most important goal is to live a life consistent with the values I hold dear and to act on what I believe in.

The people I admire most are those who have the courage of their convictions. When I attended Barry Goldwater's funeral service, I think many Republicans were surprised. (Only a few Democrats went.) They enjoyed giving me a rough time—they even gave me Goldwater's *The Conscience of a Conservative* to read on the plane. "Paul," they said, "read this—we read this book at young ages, and it set us on the right path. We still have some hope for you!" I explained that I *had* read the book at a young age—that's why I am a liberal! But I also told them that I admired Barry Goldwater for his political integrity.

I dedicate this book to, among others, Mike Epstein, who was my legislative director in Washington. Mike passed away from cancer at age sixty-three. He came to Washington almost forty years ago to work for Robert Kennedy at the Justice Department. Over time, he worked for Philip Hart, Frank Church, Robert Byrd, and Ted Kennedy, and as chief counsel of the Senate Foreign Relations Committee.

During my first year in the Senate, Mike came up to me and said, "I've been observing you. I've been here for over thirty years, but I still believe in changing the world. You need a legislative director, and I'll do it."

Mike was more than just my legislative director. He taught me the Senate rules and the legislative process, and he taught me how to be an outsider effective on the inside. Mike passionately believed in public service. "I hate this shit," Mike said of his cancer. "There is so much more I want to do." He was right: There is so much to do.

We all read about how well the economy is doing. But how can we live in the richest, most privileged country in the world, at the peak of its economic performance, and still hear from Republicans, *and too many Democrats,* that we cannot afford to provide a good education for every child, that we cannot afford to provide health security for all our citizens?

And how can it be that even with this economic performance, one out of five children under the age of six is growing up poor? Among children of color, it is even worse: one out of every three. When we allow children, our most precious yet most vulnerable citizens, to be our most poverty-stricken group, it is a national disgrace, a betrayal of our heritage.

When my first grandchild, Cari Hannah, was born nine years ago, I grasped at age forty-six the core value that informs my liberal politics. I held her in my hands, and I knew what I hoped: that every infant I hold or you hold will have the same chance to reach his or her full potential.

If we do not make good our national vow of equal opportunity for every child now, when will we?

As Cari got older, I watched her with amazement. Every fifteen seconds, she was interested in something new. Little children experience all of the unnamed magic of the world before them. They are all beautiful, and they *all* deserve our support.

Sometimes, the only realists are the dreamers. Robert Kennedy once said, "The future will not belong to those who are content with the present." I think the future also will not belong to those who are cynical or those who stand on the sidelines. The future will belong to those who have passion and are willing to work hard to make our country better. The future will belong to those, in Eleanor Roosevelt's words, "who believe in the beauty of their dreams."

In 1990, with the help of many wonderful people, I was able to defy impossible odds. Outspent by a margin of seven to one and considered a hopeless cause by the pundits, we won the U.S. Senate race in Minnesota. We didn't win by matching pollster against pollster, ad against ad, image maker against image maker. We won by *including citizens* in an inspiring grassroots campaign. Indeed, for many months after the election, Minnesotans ran up to me and said, "Paul, we are so excited. We helped you. And if you could win, anyone can!"

I had to think about that. I believe and hope this was empowerment. They were saying, People like us can win a U.S. Senate race. We *do* count in American politics.

The 1990 campaign is definitely where to begin this book.

Maybe I'm willing to believe in the impossible because I beat impossible odds.

After ten years in the U.S. Senate, I have learned a lot about politics. My Jewish guilt tells me I should probably send out a refund to the students who took my American politics class, back when I was a professor.

This book is a personal account of my political journey. But most important, it is about you. Each chapter is a call for an active citizen politics that could provide an *outside* motive for change, to make our country better. It is a huge agenda to restore democracy and build a progressive politics, especially in these times.

George W. Bush is now president, and Republicans, for the first time in half a century, control the White House and Congress. The irony is that Bush was able to win the election by focusing in part on children, education, prescription drug costs, health care, and Social Security. He described his philosophy as "compassionate conservatism." He won, in part, on Democratic, progressive issues. But his "compassionate conservatism," while praising local volunteer efforts, says there is little that government can or should do about the most pressing issues of people's lives. This is a fine philosophy if you run your own corporation and are wealthy. It does not work for most of the people.

Moreover, the real Bush agenda is now coming into sharp relief: $1.6 trillion in tax cuts targeted mainly to the wealthy; privatization of Medicare and Social Security; an attack on federal workplace health and safety efforts, as well as on the right of workers to organize and bargain collectively; an assault on the environment led by a protégée of notorious Reagan administration interior secretary James Watt; excessive and wasteful new Pentagon spending, including on national missile defenses ("Star Wars"); and a direct challenge to *Roe v. Wade* and a woman's right to choose. There is more, but this ought to be enough to galvanize progressives throughout the country.

Now is the time for progressives to thrust forward new ideas and new leaders. People yearn for a "politics of the center"—not "the center" so widely discussed by politicians and pundits in Washington but rather a politics that speaks to the center of people's lives: affordable child care, good education for children, health security, living-wage jobs that will support families, respect for the environment and human rights, and clean elections and clean campaigns.

I hope this book provides insight into how we can reclaim the politics of compassion, how government can be a force for good, and how we can improve the lives of our children, our communities, and our nation for generations to come. There is, of course, no guarantee of success. But politics is not about observations or predictions. Politics is what we create by what we do, what we hope for, and what we dare to imagine.

THE CONSCIENCE

OF A LIBERAL

Chapter 1

—

THIS TIME, VOTE

FOR WHAT YOU BELIEVE IN

I met Sheila Ison when we were both sixteen, on the beach at Ocean City, Maryland—a big high-school hangout place—right after the school year ended.

She is the daughter of Appalachian Southern Baptists. Her parents were from Harlan and Letcher counties, Kentucky— coal-mining families. When I first met them, I immediately thought of the song "Two Different Worlds." They were half my parents' age and completely different from them. Her grandfather, who was visiting when I first came to their home, even said after I left, "He is a nice boy, but he is a Jew. You wouldn't want to marry him."

But we were married just after turning nineteen. Sheila had been at the University of Kentucky, and I was at the University of

North Carolina. I told my parents in December that I was very unhappy separated from Sheila and that I wanted to marry her. Almost everyone was opposed for obvious reasons, but not my father. As usual, he could see ahead. We were married August 24, 1963.

Chapel Hill, North Carolina, was a great place to be a student. The civil rights movement was exploding all around me. At first, I was hesitant to get involved, because of time. I was married, competing as a wrestler, taking an overload of classes (I graduated a year early), working, and a father at age twenty. There was no time for political activism.

Direct action is powerful. Sheila and I saw the sit-ins—men and women, black and white, young and old, asking to be served in restaurants and instead being beaten and arrested by police. It made you think. And it made you act. I found a way to be a foot soldier in this movement—not a hero, like my present colleague John Lewis from Georgia. But we helped out in whatever ways we could and became a small part of many of the justice struggles in Chapel Hill: civil rights, antiwar, antihunger, and antipoverty work.

I did my graduate work in political science at UNC and received a doctorate at twenty-four. But I had learned a great deal in a short period of time. I met many men and women who should be famous. They had little in the way of financial resources, but they were the ones who made history. Their courage, their ability, their love made our country better, not just for people of color but for all Americans. I learned from firsthand experience that ordinary people can be extraordinary and have the capacity to make our country better. I became a believer in grassroots organizing, in grassroots politics.

I came to Carleton College in Northfield, Minnesota, in September 1969, with the knowledge that individuals can change the world. I was determined not to be an outside observer but to use my skills as a political scientist to empower people and to step forward with people in justice struggles. If this sounds a bit too romantic, remember that I was only twenty-five. And yet today I still feel the same way! We act on what we believe in where we live, where we work, or where we go to school. (I always feel the need to include students.) I organized on campus on many different issues. But most of my work was organizing with poor people in rural Rice County, Minnesota (population 41,000; 495 square miles).

First, I supervised studies of housing, health care, and nutrition needs. We identified needs but made no policy recommendations. It was controversial work. The college was not used to this kind of community research. And when it became clear that the data would be used *by* poor people *for* poor people, neither the county nor college officials were pleased. I remember one of many confrontations over this research. The then-president of Carleton said: "One would think that in good political science public-policy research, there would be a clear set of policy recommendations for the relevant decision-makers." The *untenured* assistant professor—me—replied: "This isn't for the politicians and the elite, it is for poor people that are affected by the problems. It is to help empower them to take action."

This organizing work, which I will detail later in the book, combined with my activism on campus, was too much for Carleton College. After two years, I was given a one-year contract with a warning that I would be fired if I did not change. I didn't change, and they carried through with their threat. It was a unanimous decision by the political science department, the president, the dean, and the board of trustees. I was given one year's notice. When the dean called me into his office and notified me of this decision, I was shaken. Right away, I thought of Sheila and our three children. Where would we go? What were we going to do? I felt tremendous fear and guilt. This experience gave me a real feeling for why many people put up with so much and are so passive. You do not want to lose your job. You have to put bread on the table and prioritize for your family. That is why most people, as someone once said, are more concerned with making a living than with making history.

This firing came right after I had received the best student evaluations of all third-year teachers. Lucky for me, there was a student rebellion. Fifteen hundred students out of sixteen hundred signed a petition demanding that the decision be reversed. The 150 black and Latino students (most of whom were attending Carleton through a Rockefeller grant program aimed at ghettos and barrios) all signed a separate petition and were a major force on my side. The student paper, in spite of considerable pressure, carried many strong articles and editorials of support. And an older mathematics professor, Sy Schuster, stepped forward and said he would help me.

This was a yearlong fight. The students organized, poor people in Rice County came to my support, and Sy Schuster successfully challenged some of the ways the decision had been made. The college, under tremendous pressure, agreed to bring in prominent political scientists as outside evaluators. Their evaluations were great (much more than I deserved).

But at least some trustees remained in favor of firing me. Dean Bruce Morgan, who now felt I had been wronged, threatened to resign if the board did not reverse the decision and, most important, immediately grant me tenure. He argued that I, of all professors, needed the protection of tenure. The trustees acceded to his demand.

It was amazing. In one year, I went from being fired to being the youngest (age twenty-eight) tenured professor in the history of Carleton. I owe so much to Sy Schuster and especially to the students. As one student put it to me, "Paul, you taught us how to organize, and it was a pleasure to put it into practice for you!" Last year, I spoke at the twenty-fifth reunion of this class of 1974 that saved me. There was and still is a lot of love.

—

My students have had such a formative impact on my life and work. When Jeff Blodgett was a student in my class on community organizing in 1981, he was the only student I remember who was interested in electoral politics as a way to effect social change. The rest of the class believed that organizing people for power and direct action, as in the labor movement of the 1930s and the civil rights movement of the 1960s, was the only way to succeed. They viewed running for office as a waste of time. I sided with the other students against him!

Over the years, I came around to Jeff's point of view, and nine years later he became the manager of my 1990 campaign. He again managed my 1996 campaign. It is a strange feeling to have your political life depend on former students!

My twenty years in Minnesota were a combination of teaching, writing, speaking, and community organizing. I traveled the state widely and was involved in most of the farm, labor, antipoverty, environmental, peace, and economic justice struggles. This rich experience gave me an appreciation of three critical ingredients for effective political activism: good ideas and policy, so that your activism has direction; grassroots organizing, so that there is a constituency to fight for the change; *and* electoral politics, since it is one of the ways people feel most comfortable deciding about power in our country. If I could will into existence another social movement like the labor or civil rights movement, I would do so in a second. Indeed, my intuition tells me that the next social movement will be around the right of people to organize, bargain collectively, and earn a decent standard of living so that they can give their children the care and opportunities they need and deserve.

But we act with political purpose. We do not create the winds and the tides, the conditions that give rise to great social movements. So it is important to achieve power in other ways. And in a representative democracy, it matters whom we elect to office and hold accountable for public policy. Those who eschew electoral politics marginalize themselves.

I ran for the Senate because I wanted to use this position of power to make a difference. I wanted to go to Washington to fight for the people and causes I believed in. I wanted to travel Minnesota and the country to help empower people, to nurture and support organizing and citizen politics, to engage, energize, excite, and galvanize citizens to make our country better. This was my dream.

What finally put me over the edge was my experience with students. Quite often, I was invited to speak at high schools, and each time I asked students to take out a piece of paper and write down the first words that came to mind when I mentioned the word *politics* to them. Their comments were devastating: "fake," "phony," "corrupt," "promises never kept," "big money," et cetera. Rarely was there a positive comment.

I said to students, "No, politics is not about money or power games, or winning for the sake of winning. Politics is about the improvement of people's lives, lessening human suffering, advancing the cause of peace and justice in our country and in the world."

And while I was saying this to them, I was saying to myself, "Paul, it is time to run for the Senate."

I didn't know whether I could win, but I was full of indignation. Thousands of Minnesota farmers were driven off their land in the mid-1980s by record low food prices and record debt. Some of them, whom I knew personally, took their lives. This was not inevitable; it was the result of a stacked deck.

In Austin, Minnesota, in 1985, meatpackers on strike over deplorable working conditions were crushed. The Hormel company brought in workers to permanently replace striking union members. I wish the local union, P-9, had gone back to work when the Minnesota National Guard came to Austin to ensure that Hormel could bring in the permanent replacements. My advice then was to go back to work "to be able to fight another day." But I admired their courage, and it was very painful to see them fired, to see so many broken dreams, broken families, and broken lives. I spent many days and nights on the picket line with these workers. We became close friends. I got to know their spouses and children.

These were two major political struggles in Minnesota. I was incensed that so few politicians supported the farmers and workers, especially when it came to being on the front line with them. I ran for the Senate to shake things up, especially the Democratic Party, which to me had lost its soul, its sense of justice.

I am a very confident public speaker. For me, speaking was a way to organize people. There were some interesting moments. The politics of racist and anti-Semitic hatred had moved into rural America, exploiting the farmers' desperation. Since I was the only Jew actively speaking and organizing with farmers, I mentioned my own Jewish background when appealing to the farmers to "not let the worst of times bring out the worst in you."

But the anti-Semitism was real, and I received some threatening hate mail. Close friends pleaded with me to stop speaking at farm gatherings. But when you are five feet five and a half, you don't listen to such advice. So I went to speak in Alexandria, Minnesota. My only accommodation was that I didn't mention the fact that I am Jewish.

After I spoke, a big guy approached me (a lot of guys look big to me) and asked, "What country are you from?"

"The United States," I replied.

"Where were you born?" he asked.

"Washington, D.C."

"Where are your parents from?"

"My father fled persecution in Russia, and my mother was born on the Lower East Side of New York City."

He looked at me and said, "Then you are a Jew."

I tensed up (and was ready to take him down if necessary—remember that I was a college wrestler!) and said, "Yes, I am."

He stuck out his hand and said, "Well, buddy, I'm a Finn, and we minorities have to struggle together!"

Not what I expected, but what a relief. I've loved Minnesota ever since!

I did come to realize over the years that I was blessed with one great strength: the ability to move and inspire people. I believed that I could apply my speaking and organizing to a U.S. Senate race. I thought I could raise big issues and at least come close, if not win. I ended every speech in 1989 and 1990 by saying, "This time, vote for what you believe in." These words connected especially with Democrats who wanted to be excited by a campaign, who were tired of conventional wisdom about who could win, and who figured that Rudy Boschwitz, the Republican incumbent, was, with all of his money, unbeatable. Why not go for what you believed in? First, we had to win the DFL Party endorsement in June 1990. (In Minnesota, the Democrats function as the Democratic-Farmer-Labor Party.) This process started with precinct caucuses that February, then county conventions, congressional-district conventions, and finally the state convention.

Tom Berg was the clear favorite, by conventional standards. He had had a distinguished political career: state legislator (he had the backing of almost all the DFL legislators), U.S. attorney, and campaign manager for Governor Rudy Perpich's overwhelming victory in 1986. Tom was very capable and very articulate.

Jim Nichols was also a formidable candidate. He had been a great populist agriculture commissioner and was very well known in the state.

But we knew how to organize, how to turn people out to the caucuses, and that is exactly what we did in February. Our supporters were everywhere, and we were starting out strong. I'll never forget the Minneapolis *Star Tribune* coverage: a picture of me speaking at a caucus with the headline LIBERAL LONGSHOT. It was kind of discouraging, since I thought we had such a great start.

The party-endorsement fight was to gain the support of political activists. This is living-room politics, in which you meet with small groups of people in their homes all across the state, not to mention at all the county fairs and fish-fry dinners. And you are not campaigning on a jet. You are driving through the snowstorms and winter weather to meet with ten people, maybe fifty, maybe a few more. Big money cannot dominate this process!

We had several strengths. I loved speaking and meeting with people. Chemistry still matters in politics. Stump speaking can be and was for me a way of organizing, of galvanizing our core support. This was especially important at the beginning when no one gave us a chance. People had to believe! I would say, "The communist Soviet Union is changing, the Berlin Wall has come toppling down, Václav Havel, the imprisoned playwright, is now the president of Czechoslovakia. If all that can happen, then surely we can beat Rudy Boschwitz and win the U.S. Senate race in Minnesota!" People loved it.

All the activists I had worked with over twenty years—poor people, farmers, workers, environmentalists, the peace and justice community, teachers, neighborhood activists, and students— became involved in the campaign. They were the volunteers, the great organizers. They were the core, the energy. Every campaign, to be successful, has to start out with a circle of people who believe. Of course, the circle has to get wider and wider. Then there were all the students I gave A's to over the years! (I'm kidding.)

The third factor was Gabe Brisbois. Gabe was a great junior high schoolteacher in Hibbing, on the Iron Range. The Mesabi Iron Range, in northeast Minnesota, is overwhelmingly eastern European and working-class. The largest union is of steelworkers in the iron ore mines. The people take their freedom (given their immigrant backgrounds) and politics very seriously. Their vote often determines a Democratic primary, with an 80 percent turnout in the region. In the general election, the turnout can be above 90 percent! People on the Range said that Gabe Brisbois never lost. It was an exaggeration, but his reputation as someone you had to have on your side was well deserved.

Gabe and his wife, Mary Ann, told me when I first called them for their support that they had made an extra key to their house, which I was to make my home while on the Range. I made the final decision to run for the Senate in their Iron Range home on March 31, 1989. This was critically important because I had to have strong support on the Range. (The usual split in the DFL Party is between "metro liberal" and "greater [rural] Minnesota.")

One night around eleven-thirty, we were sitting in Gabe's kitchen talking. It had been a long day of campaigning, and we were unwinding. I said to Gabe, "You should write a book about Iron Range politics. It would be fascinating." He looked at me, his expression changed, and he replied, "Not me, I'm just a junior high teacher. I'm not a historian, I can't write a book." I was shocked to hear this. "Gabe," I said, "of course you could. You know more than anyone about Range politics." He said quietly, "You don't understand. Even when you are almost fifty, you never regain confidence after they take you as a kid out of your home, away from your reservation, and send you to boarding school." He studied me carefully. "You didn't know I'm an American Indian, did you?"

Now I understood why I was given the key to Gabe's home:

"Gabe, you have all this quiet indignation, and you want to turn things upside down. So do I." This was a key moment in our journey together and in what has become an unyielding friendship. With Gabe, it was all labor-intensive politics. WELLSTONE FOR SENATE lawn signs cropped up all across the Range, including choice highway locations, long before those of other candidates. Gabe made sure our signs were in before the ground froze in the late fall of 1989.

Gabe was a critical partner in our victory. Two other great friends were (and still are) as important to me as he is. Sam and Sylvia Kaplan, two prominent businesspeople and highly influential Democrats in the Twin Cities, were two of the few "heavy hitters" who supported my candidacy and gave me a chance to win. We first met at Sam's law office on the fifty-fifth floor of the Norwest tower in downtown Minneapolis. I knew Sam was the "Cadillac of lawyers" in Minnesota, that he and Sylvia were real power brokers, but I had never in my life met two people like them. The more we talked, however, the more we actually liked one another. We believed in the same progressive politics. They were stalwart liberals who favored universal health care coverage and progressive taxes. Though they are wealthy, Sam and Sylvia have always been strong advocates for campaign finance reform. Most important, they were tired of timid politics. I couldn't believe how much they wanted to shake things up. After two hours of discussion, we believed in one another. Their early support sent a strong signal to the political class in Minnesota that our campaign was serious.

Then there was café politics. I'd go to cafés at breakfast and at lunchtime, sitting down at tables and booths, asking people to tell me what issues they cared most about. I asked, "If you were in my shoes, running against a well-entrenched incumbent with millions of dollars, which issues would you focus on?" I learned about cafés from Rudy Perpich, who was from the Range. He had said to me early in 1989, "I know you are a professor and will be tempted to talk about all kinds of issues. Don't! Go into cafés, and listen to people, and then make it simple. Remember my campaigns. It was 'Perpich=Jobs,' no ten-point program."

The café discussions were great on the Iron Range and also, later, throughout Minnesota. They helped me focus on a few key issues, such as health care, education and children, and the influence of big money on politics. Of course, these had always been priority issues to me, but I needed to hear them from people in their own voices. I was always energized by these discussions, and I was able to repeat the stories people had told me about their struggles and concerns. This was language that connected to the voters.

These café meetings defined the populist style of our campaign. I generally didn't do interviews in newspaper offices and radio stations. They came to cover me in the cafés. People on the Iron Range and in rural Minnesota and elsewhere loved it, and so did I.

Finally, we needed strong and early support from the steelworkers. They were impressed when I showed up over and over again early in the morning to shake hands at the plant gates. And since I had over the years come to labor gatherings, stood on the picket lines with workers, and left no doubt "whose side I was on," the locals on the Range gave me early endorsements and demanded their union get behind me. I don't think most of the workers thought I had any chance of winning, but they were in a fighting mood.

This was grassroots politics: lawn signs, cafés, house meetings, local endorsements, many personal phone calls, and many small-dollar fund-raisers. I remember vividly a fund-raiser put on mainly by welfare mothers, with potluck casseroles bought with food stamps. These women believed I would represent them and for the first time were involved in politics.

Dennis McGrath and Dane Smith, two fine journalists with the Minneapolis *Star Tribune,* wrote a book about this 1990 Senate race titled *Professor Wellstone Goes to Washington.* As part of his research, Dane Smith called Gabe Brisbois to talk about this campaign. About fifteen minutes into the interview, Gabe said to Dane, "I'm pleased to answer your questions, but let me also give you the names of many other people who were the foundations of the campaign."

Dane said, "Thank you, but I really don't have the time to interview all of them."

Gabe responded, "You will never understand how grassroots this campaign was, even poor people contributing meals bought by food stamps, unless you interview people."

"I know," Dane said, "but I just don't have the time."

At which point Gabe Brisbois said, "Then I don't want anything to do with your book," and hung up on him.

I know about this because Dane Smith called me, shocked by what had just happened.

It was simple. Gabe believed that McGrath and Smith were convinced that our victory was the result of a few brilliant strategists making it all happen. He disagreed with this analysis and felt it was a false picture of what really happened. Gabe wanted to focus on grassroots leaders.

We also had surprisingly strong support in the farm communities. A liberal Democrat was not supposed to do well with the more conservative rural Democrats, but I had been on the side of family farmers and rural communities for years. Long before even considering a Senate race, I had organized with farmers in the early and mid-1980s. There were what seemed like a million meetings, many rallies (including one with ten thousand farmers and rural people in January 1985), and too many farm foreclosures. I'll never forget one of the many farm gatherings at the state legislature. A farmer came up to me and asked the question he had been wanting to ask for a long time: "Do you have a job?" He had seen me everywhere and wanted to know how I was able to miss work so often.

I told him I was a college teacher and that I had classes Monday, Wednesday, and Friday all morning and on Tuesday and Thursday afternoons. But, I went on, there are office hours and the time spent preparing for classes and grading papers. I could tell by the farmer's smile that he thought I had a pretty good deal!

For one year (1983–1984), however, I had a different job: special assistant to Governor Perpich. That period saw the most controversial moment of my activism, when I was arrested with family farmers in Paynesville. The First National Bank, Paynesville, had called in the demand note on the Kohnen dairy farm. Land values had plummeted, and therefore the farm's debt-to-asset ratio had changed dramatically. The bank said the farm was no longer solvent, and it intended to foreclose. At the first sign of trouble, this huge branch bank wanted out of its farm loans. Farmers then organized an "action" on the bank: They marched into the bank with the Kohnen family and demanded negotiations.

A former student of mine, Joel Chrastil, asked me to come to Paynesville to support this effort. When I left home, Sheila said to me, "Don't get arrested!"

I said, "Of course not, don't worry about it. I am working for the governor. I certainly can't get arrested." Famous last words!

Sheila knew me too well. The problem is, I made the mistake of jumping on a table and giving a speech about how we would "stay until there is justice for the Kohnen family." I thought the bank would surely work out a compromise.

But not so. At closing time, one of the farmers, Mike Laidlaw, announced, "Some of us are staying!" They turned to me to ask what I was going to do. I had no choice. I'd given the speech! I couldn't walk out on the farmers or him. I made the lead story on the 6:00 and 10:00 P.M. news, being handcuffed and led away by the police. Not a good move for a special assistant to the governor and not a great strategy for getting elected to the U.S. Senate.

This arrest came up several times shortly before the Democratic Party convention in June 1990. But it never hurt and may have even helped. In any case, I was never convicted, since the bank was not eager to go to trial. In fact, I was disappointed since (in my not-so-humble opinion) I had a great statement ready to put *them* on trial.

As the campaign heated up in April and May, I focused on populist economic issues. At all the different district party conventions, we tried to excite and galvanize people. Indeed, the party activists were enjoying the campaign. They liked being fired up. It was fun. I also think the campaign, full of idealism and hope, reminded them of why they became involved in politics in the first place.

I remember one congressional district convention in Bemidji, in northwest Minnesota. After I spoke, there was a rousing response. People were on their feet and cheering. It was great. One of my opponents spoke next. He lectured everyone not to get excited and emotional but to focus on substance and on who really had the stature and best chance to win. This lecture not to feel good or get excited about politics didn't go over well. The debates were fierce. My opponents and almost all the "influential" people in the party attacked me for being too liberal, too radical, and not electable. I criticized what I called their "tippy-toe" politics. I didn't pull any punches on universal health care, the right to organize, living-wage jobs, and the evil influence of big money in politics. Only a rock-the-boat, populist, fun, exciting campaign could win, I argued.

The DFL Party rules required that a nominee receive the votes of 60 percent of the approximately 1,200 delegates. On the seventh ballot, we were endorsed.

It was an exciting victory. We beat two superb candidates in Tom Berg and Jim Nichols. We beat many of the "investors and heavy hitters" in the DFL who were adamantly opposed, and we won with many labor union leaders still in opposition. The grassroots activists, the organizers, the rank-and-file union members won the party endorsement. They were determined this time to vote for what they believed in.

The party endorsement was critical for someone like me who was not wealthy, not well known, and in need of organized support. Walter Dean Burnham, an eminent political scientist, has written that political parties, with all their imperfections, are still the only institutions in a representative democracy in which ordinary people who don't have the capital can aggregate and make a difference. Our campaign proved this.

Jim Nichols decided to challenge the party endorsement and

enter a primary. We were disheartened. The primary wouldn't be decided until September 4, the first Tuesday after Labor Day, and this left precious little time to challenge a two-term incumbent with millions of dollars and an 80 percent approval rating.

As it turns out, the primary was the best thing that could have happened for us, thanks to the work of Pat Forceia, who helped manage the campaign. This was no longer competition for a small universe of delegate votes. We were forced to organize a field operation—voter registration, voter identification, get-out-the-vote operations, and advertising—something that I didn't want to think about.

Bill Hillsman, who had been a student at Carleton College, arranged a meeting with his friends in advertising who were potentially interested in helping the campaign. I told them how much I hated political advertising. As a political scientist, I thought it was the worst part of American politics—fake, empty, manipulative, and vicious. I wasn't sure I wanted anything to do with it.

Their response surprised me. They wanted to know who I was, what I believed in, why I was running, and why I wanted to be a senator. They also wanted to know whether this would be a serious effort to win. Otherwise, they said, "Why waste our time?"

There was only one woman at this meeting. After listening to me respond to the questions, she said, "You can win. You are so personal and sincere, and you will connect with people, and we will respect your wishes with our ads. I promise you, they will make you proud." It was because of what she said that I agreed to ads (what few we could afford). The ads became, I am embarrassed to say, a major factor in our final victory.

With one week to go before the primary, a St. Paul *Pioneer Press* poll showed me six points behind. You worry polls like this will cause people to vote against you, since conventional wisdom says people like to be with the winner. Fortunately, the poll was way off. We had built a great grassroots organization, and the poll did not measure turnout, an especially crucial factor in a primary. We won by twenty-two points! This victory was a huge step for us. Since the media had more or less dismissed the campaign as hopeless, we had to prove that we could win a race with voters, not just with party activists at a convention. Our decisive victory brought respect.

This was also the first time, after a year of campaigning, that I was live on all the TV stations for the 10:00 P.M. news. In a hotel room packed with people, most of them students and very young, I started out the victory speech this way: "To all the students and young people that are here: Politics is not about money and power games. It is about improving people's lives, about making our country better. Thank you for all your support."

This was a critical message. I wanted our campaign to speak to and include young people. I wanted a campaign infused with idealism. The students would be our army of volunteer organizers, *and* through them I would get to the parents in the suburbs. Parents, I believed, would be excited and positive to see their kids excited and positive, not cynical. This was my honest-to-God strategy for winning in the suburbs. And it worked!

Vice President Walter Mondale called me after our subsequent victory in November. He said, "Your campaign was the first campaign I've seen since George McGovern in 1972 and Bobby

Kennedy and Gene McCarthy in 1968 that really turned the students on. They carried you on their shoulders to victory." It is true. And the same thing happened in 1996.

One funny thing happened on the night of the primary that was very significant. Sheila spoke—with all the cameras staring her in the face—live on television. She had no notes, and I was a nervous wreck. I was sure she would go blank. But when she started to speak, her words and style were powerful. In twenty-seven years of marriage, I had never really heard her give a public speech. I'll confess that rather than just being very proud of her, I was thinking, "This is gold. I am going to have her everywhere in the campaign." Even if you're idealistic, politics can make you calculating! Sheila has campaigned and worked with me every single day from that night.

Rudy Boschwitz must have been delighted the night we won the primary. He had a dream opponent: a short, little-known college professor with next to no money who was *a liberal*.

My trips to Washington, D.C., as the Democratic candidate from Minnesota were a disaster. I met with Senator John Breaux, chair of the Democratic Senatorial Campaign Committee (DSCC), and explained to him how we would win: an all-out grassroots campaign in an old green bus, lots of volunteers, café politics, populist economics, and campaigning against big-money politics. John (whom I like and whose company I enjoy) wanted to know how much money I had raised. That was the end of the conversation.

There were only two Democratic senators who had the time to meet with me. Political reporters who were supposed to meet me didn't show up. The AFL-CIO leadership seemed disinterested in a long-shot candidate.

Visiting Washington made me feel small, and I vowed never to return.

But of course I did return—for the DSCC gala, where I was to meet potential donors. We needed money. It was one of the most humiliating experiences of my life. Here was the methodology: Our fund-raiser would say, "Joe Smith is at table twelve, he has lots of money and might be willing to support you." He would then point me in the right direction, give a push, and off I went. I even saw some great senators getting the same shove. After a few rounds of this, I became physically ill. I left the gathering and went back to Minnesota empty.

Then there was the Minnesota challenge. The investors in the DFL Party were not happy with me as their candidate. My positions on just about every issue—health care, trade, taxes, agriculture, defense spending, the environment, labor organizing—had not endeared me to them. So again the big problem was money. And prestige. There were too many private and public quotes that this campaign was a "suicide mission." It didn't help that initially I was behind by about thirty points!

How did we win? Let me start with that old 1967 school bus, painted green by United Auto Workers supporters. Mike Casper—a physics professor and my best friend at Carleton—and I ran every day at noon and tried to plan the campaign. Our idea was to find a bus with a speaking platform on the back so we could have a Harry Truman–like campaign, with a bus rather than a train.

This bus was not fancy. We didn't even have a bathroom that worked. Before we purchased it, one group of friends argued that the bus would break down all the time (and it did) and that journalists would report that the broken-down bus was a metaphor for the campaign. But we had to take chances, and I felt the bus would be a powerful symbol for a grassroots, David vs. Goliath, galvanizing campaign.

The stump speaking from the platform was a miserable failure. My idea was that we would pull up into a small town, and I would start speaking, and people would gather around. The only problem was that most people, not knowing who the hell I was, ran in the opposite direction. I can and love to speak, but old-fashioned stump speaking is out of fashion in America. People are not used to it and don't know how to react to it. It is kind of a sad commentary on contemporary politics, since speaking and meeting with people is a lot more real than all the phony ads on television.

The bus became bigger than life. When it broke down on the highway, people would honk their horns and smile or get out and help. Fortunately, Paul Scott, our driver (a former Greyhound bus driver) could usually get us back on the road again. With each passing week, the bus evoked more and more of a response. Horns honked everywhere. People gathered around wherever we stopped. Parents brought their children on the bus for a tour! The bus was a rejection of slick, big-money politics, and Minnesotans loved it.

We certainly didn't have the money, so we had to turn this into a plus. I truly hate to admit it, but our television ads made a real difference. A small budget meant we had to get a lot of bang for our buck. Bill Hillsman and crew went to work.

The first ad, called "Fast-Paced Paul," was risky. I started off standing in front of the bus, said I didn't have much money and would have to talk fast, and then raced from school to farm to hospital to labor hall to announce my positions, and then jumped onto the bus and sped off. It was very "unsenatorial." And we knew Minnesotans would either say, "We don't want this clown as a senator," or they would laugh, smile, and love it, which is what happened. The ad was the talk of Minnesota. The next ad was even better. It was titled "Looking for Rudy." We wanted debates, but the Boschwitz campaign didn't, given their huge lead. Patterned after Michael Moore's movie *Roger and Me,* the ad showed me looking for Rudy Boschwitz so I could ask him to debate me. We went to his campaign offices, businesses he owned, everywhere, looking for him. There was no script. We asked Boschwitz's staff where he was, and whether they agreed we should have some debates. They were surprised, and in front of the cameras they didn't know what to say. The wonderful thing is that we kept getting different stories in different places as to where we could find Senator Boschwitz. The ad was not vicious, but it was hilarious.

It ran for two minutes, and we had the money to run it only once, but it was so different, so unique, and so effective that newscasts showed it over and over again. I remember when I knew this was a home run. I was driving one early morning in rural Minnesota, late for a gathering. I had to stop in a small café and use the bathroom. My plan was to slip in and out. As I was rushing out of the café, a group of farmers having coffee yelled out, "Have you found Rudy?" and they roared with laughter.

Most important, the ad and reaction forced the Boschwitz campaign into a debate. They demanded I go to Washington for it because Senator Boschwitz was too busy with budget work to come to Minnesota. It was a curious decision on their part, since it enabled me to go "look for Rudy" in Washington and generated much more interest in the debate.

I've never been more nervous than before this October television debate. This was the whole campaign, because this was the first and perhaps only opportunity to cut into his huge lead. If I did poorly, the campaign was over.

Maybe the best decision I made was right before the debate started, when technicians in the studio insisted I stand on a riser. Otherwise, they explained, Boschwitz, who is more than six feet tall, would tower over me, and I would look weak. I told them I intended to win this race on my own terms, including my height. What I also was thinking was that being a little guy (literally) would only help in this underdog campaign. I still reject risers unless I literally cannot see over the podium!

I can't honestly say I dominated the debate. But I did establish a theme, since I described every one of his answers as "a Washington answer," opposed to Minnesota values. This debate was a huge step forward for us. It demonstrated the power and positive potential of television. Twenty-three percent of eligible Minnesota voters are estimated to have watched the debate. For the first time, they learned who I was and what some of my positions on issues are. Grassroots politics I love, but you can meet only so many people face-to-face. The debate introduced me to Minnesotans, and a few days later the polls showed me only fourteen points behind. Rudy Boschwitz's lead had been cut by more than half!

The excitement built. There were more debates (two on radio and one on public television), now closely followed. We crisscrossed Minnesota in the green bus, and crowds were everywhere. Volunteers poured into the campaign office. We had momentum.

The Boschwitz campaign struck back. They had the money—seven million dollars—for unlimited attack ads. The most devastating ad shown in the final two weeks accused me of wanting to take away Medicare coverage from senior citizens.

It was a diabolically clever ad. Since I was for universal coverage, they decided it was fair to say that I was against separate Medicare coverage. It seemed like every fifteen seconds, from early in the morning to late at night, there would be an elderly woman asking, "Who is this man who wants to eliminate my Medicare?" Then my face would appear on the screen. My name would be repeated over and over again as the man who wanted to take away Medicare. One press conference at a senior center was no match for this barrage.

Almost all of the time, when you are outspent by a seven-to-one margin, you lose. Your opponent attacks and attacks on television, and you are defenseless. But we had galvanized people. Neighbors were going door-to-door to support us. Indeed, there were enough volunteers to drop literature late Monday night so that early Tuesday morning, Election Day, every resident of Minneapolis and St. Paul—more than six hundred thousand people—would be greeted with a piece of literature. There was massive involvement of people everywhere in Minnesota.

The critical day, however, was the Friday three days before the election. I was flying around the state. The attacks were fast and furious. At one stop, the charge was that I wanted to take everyone's gun away. (Minnesota is a big hunting state.) Next stop, it was that I favored abortion at nine months for the purpose of sex selection. Then we arrived back in St. Paul at 6:00 P.M. to be confronted with another kind of attack. The Boschwitz camp had sent a letter to the Jewish community suggesting that I was not a good Jew since I was married to a Christian. The media had obtained the letter and surrounded me as soon as I got off the plane.

I requested a few minutes to read this letter. I also put in a quick call to Sam and Sylvia Kaplan. Sam said, "Paul, Rudy Boschwitz has raised one of the most sensitive issues in the Jewish community. This is unconscionable."

Sheila was with me. There were tears in her eyes. She was always so worried about somehow hurting my chance to win, and now she blamed herself. This was a very emotional moment. I had tears in my eyes, tears of anger.

I returned to the media for the most dramatic press conference of the campaign. I looked in the cameras and said, "I guess Senator Boschwitz is criticizing me for marrying a Christian." I was not in the mood for a philosophical discussion; I wanted to take this scum attack and cram it down Boschwitz's throat. That is the way I felt. And I was fully aware that most Minnesotans are Christians, of one denomination or another.

All hell broke loose over the weekend. We may have been a little behind or a little ahead by Friday. The "Jewish letter" backfired. Many Minnesotans were angry about it, and it helped push us over the top. By about 10:00 P.M. on Tuesday night, we had won, 51 percent to 49 percent. It was an amazing, stunning upset victory.

People were so excited. As one woman hugged me, she said, "You are the first person I've voted for in years who actually won!" I looked at her and replied, "*I'm* the first person I've voted for in years who actually won!"

Chapter 2

—

HOT TEA

AND SPONGE CAKE

AT 10:00 P.M.

Politics is not about left, right, or center. It is about speaking to the concerns and circumstances of people's lives. One issue that matters greatly to people is health care; almost everyone has had it affect their lives. It certainly has mine, starting with my parents.

My mother and father were an embarrassment to me, up until high school. They were much older than my friends' parents (my dad was forty-seven and my mother was forty-four when I was born), and they were from a different background, too. My mother, Minnie, was born on the Lower East Side of New York City, the daughter of Jewish immigrants from Ukraine. My father, Leon, fled persecution in Russia and came to the United States when he was seventeen, three years before the Russian Revolution. He never saw his family again.

I was ashamed of my mother for all the wrong reasons. She was a cafeteria worker at Williamsburg Junior High in Arlington, Virginia. Kids would make fun of these low-income, working-class women—especially their looks and the way they talked. I didn't want my friends to know that they were making fun of my mother.

Of course later on—much later on—I came to cherish my mother, to love her for how hard she worked to take care of me, to appreciate her obvious working-class background (the ultimate compliment my mother could pay a person was "She is a good worker"), and to deeply resent elitist put-downs of ordinary people. Now, as a senator, I insist on meeting the food-service workers at every school I visit. It is my way of honoring my mother.

With my father, it was different. By age and appearance, he just didn't fit in. And his immigrant background could cause frustrations for me as a kid. I remember once asking him to come watch me play football. I was eleven. He came and in his typical fashion stood alone, in his overcoat and hat, and left early. I scored three touchdowns.

I came home, and there he was in his small study. "Dad," I shouted out, "what did you think?"

He was completely confused: "I thought you said it was *futbol.*"

"It *was* football," I replied.

"But it was not *futbol.*"

We went round and round for about ten minutes, before I realized that football to him was soccer, the game he grew up loving in Russia.

By high school age, I came to treasure my parents, especially my father. He spoke ten languages fluently. Most important, he was a fountain of wisdom and knowledge. Every night, Sunday through

Thursday (not the weekends!), I sat with him in our tiny kitchen. We had hot tea and sponge cake, and I listened to him talk about the world—all about books, ideas, writing, knowledge, and education. It is not surprising I became a college teacher. I learned about persecution, about the importance of personal independence and human rights, to love the First Amendment, and to love our country. And, not surprisingly, I became an internationalist, interested in the world. Combined with my mother's passion for workers and for fighting for the underdog, you pretty much have the making of a life and a philosophy!

My parents were to teach me one very painful lesson. And it had to do with the miserable failure of our health care system to provide and deliver affordable and humane treatment.

We moved my parents to Northfield, Minnesota, to help take care of them. My dad, at age eighty, had advanced Parkinson's disease, and his doctors were telling me that he and my mom (who herself had a less advanced form of Parkinson's) would be better off in a nursing home. My parents still wanted to live on their own, and we—Sheila and I were thirty-three, and our children were thirteen, ten, and seven—were determined to help.

These proved to be very difficult years with my parents. Rarely, if ever, could we leave town. I am so glad, however, that our children had the opportunity to know and help take care of their grandparents. Sheila and I and our oldest son, David, rotated spending the night with them. People in Northfield, especially at the familyrun Quality Bakery and at Jacobsen's department store, were so very kind to them. This is why I love Northfield. My best moment at Carleton College came when, completely exhausted and not knowing what else to do, I sent a note to students asking whether a few of them might be willing to help us help my parents by spending a few nights with them every week. The next day, 170 students wrote back to volunteer! Several wonderful students helped us for the next year.

But then my dad fell and broke his hip. We rushed him late at night by ambulance forty-five miles to the University of Minnesota Hospital. "Give me a pill, this is vanity money," my dad told the doctors before surgery.

They turned to me, "What did he say?" (His speech was slurred as a result of Parkinson's.)

I told them, "You don't want to know."

They insisted.

"My dad," I said with tears in my eyes, "wants a pill to end his life. He does not want his meager savings for his grandchildren's college education, which means everything to him, to be wiped out by health care costs. My life, he is saying to you, is not worth it, not if it means losing all my savings for my grandchildren."

There was, for a moment, complete silence. We all knew that my father was right about health care costs and what an injustice it was that this should be his concern rather than his own life. But we went ahead, and I prayed for successful surgery.

After a month in the hospital and wonderful care, social workers again recommended putting my dad in a nursing home. Again, we were determined to keep him at home. But it was a losing struggle. My mother, even with all our help, could not take care of my father. The physical demands were too great. I felt I had no choice but to put him in a nursing home in Northfield.

We visited every day, but I felt utterly defeated. I had been so determined that my father always be able to stay at home.

My dad continued to decline. He could no longer walk and could barely talk, but he fought the disease every day. I can still see him hunched over his typewriter, his hand shaking uncontrollably, trying to write, to no avail. One day, my dad pulled me close to him so I could hear his barely audible voice: "I intensely want to die."

I was visiting students in an urban-studies program in Chicago when Sheila called me. My dad had pneumonia but was refusing to eat or take any medicine. His defiance was his dignity. The nurses knew this. They loved and respected my father and wanted to know what to do.

I wish to God I had not had to make this decision. I told them not to treat my dad, to respect his choice, that he had told me he did not want to live any longer with Parkinson's.

I flew back to Northfield and rushed to the hospital. My dad had lapsed into a coma. I stayed in his room with him. It had been several days since he had refused treatment, and though I had never been with a person who was dying, I could tell from his breathing that the time was near. I came to his bed and held him in my arms. He opened his eyes, looked up at me. Tears streamed down his cheeks. He passed away.

This was February 23, 1983. I miss my dad so much. He was the wisest, most profound person I've ever known in my life. He is in my prayers every day.

If only he could have been alive when I was elected to the Senate and been there for the swearing-in ceremony. It would have meant everything to him.

I do not understand why we as a community—a national community—do not make it our goal that older Americans and people with disabilities be able to live at home in as near normal circumstances as possible for as long as possible. This is a matter of dignity. When you get older, wouldn't you want to be able to stay at home, even in declining health? The nightmare for older people is that they will be put in a nursing home and lose all their independence, as well as their savings.

We looked for support for my dad, but it wasn't there. There should be a range of support services at the community level: regular nurse visits, neighbors trained to help, skilled home health care workers, all backed by the appropriate health care specialists. We should invest in home health care as a far preferable alternative to nursing homes.

And when nursing home care is necessary, then the staff should be paid decent wages with decent benefits, and they should be highly trained and valued for their important work. All too often, their wages are miserable, there are no health care benefits, the staff is ill-trained, there is low morale and high turnover, and the care is horrible.

We say that we value our children, the very young, and the elderly who are infirm and struggling with illness. These are our most vulnerable citizens. And yet we devalue the work of those adults who care for children and the elderly. This is an indictment of our society, of our politics. Hubert Humphrey said, "The moral test of government is how that government treats those who are in the dawn of life, the children; those who are in the twilight of life, the elderly; and those who are in the shadows of life, the sick, the needy, and the handicapped." We as a nation have failed that moral test.

Health care is a very personal issue. I was at a farm rally, heading for the speakers' platform, when Jan stopped me. "Paul," she said, "do you remember my husband, Craig? He is a railroad worker, and you met him a year ago. We told you then that he has cancer. The doctors said my Craig would only live six months [he was forty-three]. But he is a fighter." Craig was there, and Jan asked me to walk over and say hello to him. He was in a wheelchair and welcomed me warmly. He kidded around and was doing everything possible to put up a brave front.

Jan then took me aside where Craig couldn't hear and said, "It is a living hell. Every day, I'm on the phone trying to find out what the insurance company will cover. Every day, I have to fight with them for Craig's care."

No American who is struggling with an illness or has a loved one who is ill should have to go through this, to worry whether or not they can afford health care. There should be affordable, dignified, and humane health care for every American citizen.

We may not have heard much about it since Congress debated health care in 1994, but health security remains a major concern for many Americans. For some, it is a crisis that walks into their living rooms and stares them in the face. The stories go like this:

"Senator, my daughter is a diabetic. When she graduated from the university and turned twenty-two, she was taken off our coverage. It is not that they deny her coverage. But the premium is ten thousand dollars a year, and she just can't afford it."

Or, "Senator, my company downsized last year and let many of us go. I was fifty-eight. The problem is that I had cancer several years ago and now I can't find any affordable coverage. Because of the cancer, they want me to pay twelve thousand dollars a year for coverage. How can I afford that?"

When I am in cafés, I always make sure to go to the kitchen and thank the workers for the good food. I remember talking with a small group of employees at a locally owned café when the owner came in. She said, "Senator, I want you to know I can't afford to provide coverage for them. You want the proof? I can't afford to provide coverage for myself."

When elderly people are cutting their pills in half because they can't afford prescription drugs, and when the percentage of the nonelderly lacking insurance is rising, then you know that something is terribly wrong.

A trip to Houston in June 2000 provided powerful testimony about our health care crisis. I held a hearing with Congresswoman Sheila Jackson-Lee on mental health and children. The room was packed with parents desperate to tell their stories.

The most jarring words, however, came from the director of the Harris County juvenile corrections system. (Harris County is the fifth-largest county in the country.) After making clear his no-nonsense, law-and-order philosophy, he said, "A lot of people think that if these kids are locked up they did something bad to deserve it and should be locked up. The truth is that forty percent of them struggle with mental health problems, and the reason they are incarcerated is that the parents couldn't get any help for their illness. The only way the parents could get any treatment for the kids was to see them locked up." This is today, in America!

Today, more than forty-five million Americans are uninsured. Every year for more than a decade, about a million more people have been dropped from coverage. With health care costs and insurance premiums rising faster than wages, and with employers asking workers to shoulder more and more of the cost of insurance, we can expect the future to look still worse. Even assuming good economic times, close to forty-eight million Americans will have no health insurance coverage by 2005.

The uninsured and the underinsured are caught in between the existing options. They are not old enough for Medicare, they are not poor enough for medical assistance, and they are not fortunate enough to have a job that gives them decent coverage.

A rural Minnesotan speaks for a lot of people. His employer, a small business, doesn't provide health care coverage. But he wonders why he pays taxes and is a responsible member of society yet can't go to the doctor, nor can his wife and daughter, for the care they need. He asks:

> We have national health care for seniors and people with disabilities through Medicare, and we have national health care for people who are destitute through Medicaid, but for a working guy who doesn't make enough to buy his own policy and whose employer doesn't provide it, we have nothing. . . . Why do they take away our dignity and our last dime before they give us any help?

Employers used to do more. In 1985, nearly two thirds of businesses with one hundred or more workers paid the full cost of health coverage. A decade later, only one third of businesses did. In 1988, employers asked workers to pay on average 13 percent of the cost through payroll deductions. By 1996, they had raised the average worker's share to 22 percent. As health care costs escalate, the situation gets worse.

Going without health insurance means living in poorer health. Most uninsured adults have no regular source of health care. Most postpone getting care. Three in ten go without needed medical care. A quarter forgo the medicine they need because they cannot afford to fill the prescriptions. Uninsured children are 30 percent more likely to fall behind on well-child care and 80 percent more likely to never have routine care at all. Many health care providers order fewer or different treatments for patients without insurance. The uninsured are three to four times more likely to have problems getting the health care they need. Uninsured children are at least 70 percent more likely not to get medical care for common conditions—such as asthma—that if left untreated can lead to more serious health problems. Uninsured Americans are more likely to end up hospitalized for conditions—such as uncontrolled diabetes—that they could have avoided with better health care. While barely one in ten insured Americans under sixty-five is in fair to poor health, one in six of the uninsured are. In the end, uninsured patients are more likely to die while hospitalized than are privately insured patients with the same health problems. Partly because they are less likely to get regular mammograms, uninsured women are nearly 50 percent more likely to die of breast cancer. Our system takes its toll in senseless, random pain and suffering.

Too many uninsured Americans are forced to seek care in hospital emergency rooms, which cannot provide follow-up care and which are much more expensive than preventive services in a doctor's office, adding to the nation's health care bills. Taxpayers, insured Americans, and health care providers foot the bill when uninsured patients use more expensive care and when medical bills go unpaid.

Without insurance, the medical bills mount quickly. The uninsured are three times more likely to have problems with their medical bills than the insured. Eight out of ten uninsured people receive absolutely no reduced-charge or free health services. The crushing weight of bankruptcy looms on the horizon.

Even those who have insurance often struggle beneath overwhelming financial burdens. Look at the share of income that an average family has to spend on premiums and out-of-pocket payments for health care. At the bottom end of the income ladder, families with annual incomes of thirty thousand dollars or less are spending an inordinate share of their income on health care expenses. And the average family with an income under ten thousand dollars is paying well over 20 percent of its annual income. These families can least afford to make that kind of payment.

For families with annual incomes of thirty thousand dollars or more, the average amount spent on premiums, deductibles, and co-payments is below 5 percent. But this is just an average: Many families at every income level spend more than 10 percent of their income on health care, especially if someone in the family has a serious illness.

Around the country, many elderly Americans are spending well over 30 percent of their monthly budget just on prescription drugs. More than one in ten Medicare beneficiaries and nearly one in five of those in fair or poor health pay more than one hundred dollars a month out of their own pockets for their medications. Elderly patients frequently pay thousands of dollars a year for drugs. The average elderly American takes eighteen prescription drugs a year, and one third to one half of the people on Medicare have to pay for their prescriptions entirely on their own. It is wrong to force elderly women and men to have to choose between food and medicine, between heat and the prescriptions they need to live.

Throughout the country, elderly people speak with desperation about the burden of prescription costs. They are pleading for something to be done. We should expand Medicare to cover prescription drug costs.

President Clinton was right to call for this expansion of benefits in his 1999 State of the Union address. Drug companies are wrong to oppose it. The pharmaceutical industry fears that a Medicare drug benefit would hamper its ability to charge premium prices. It tells you something about how the industry exploits vulnerable consumers when it does not even want insurance to pay for the products out of fear that a strong consumer force might constrain its profits. And the politicians will not ignore the drug makers, who gave almost ten million dollars to candidates and parties in the 1998 election cycle.

Many Western nations have long provided this coverage. And drugs cost 30 percent to 100 percent more here than in many foreign countries. The Minnesota Senior Federation charters buses to Canada because people can get some drugs there for one fifth of their American price. When they look at pharmaceutical industry profits, when they look at what they are being charged, and when they look at what one can get in another country, they feel completely ripped off, and they *should!* They see excessive profit made off of the illness and misery of people, and it's wrong.

I remember vividly the words of a World War II veteran at a senior center in Minneapolis. He was taking two medications for a heart condition. But he couldn't afford to buy both drugs, so he cut the pills in half, or he took one pill one day and the other pill the next. He didn't know what else he could do. He asked why his neighbor could get prescription drugs so much cheaper by driving up to Canada.

President Clinton promised "economic security for the elderly" in his 2000 State of the Union address. The polls show (no surprise) that long-term care is a big concern to American families. But he was afraid to propose a bold government program. So instead, senior citizens will receive a tax credit of up to three thousand dollars per year. This is a cruel joke. My parents, like most elderly Americans, never could have afforded to stay at home with only three thousand dollars to pay for services.

Too many Democrats learned the wrong lessons from the 1993–1994 health care battle. They think the only way to go is in small steps acceptable to vested health care interests. The truth is we need bold proposals that will really help people and that an aroused public will fight for.

Health security for all Americans is an idea whose time has come.

When Bill Clinton was elected president, I was full of hope. Arthur Schlesinger's cycles of history seemed to apply. Just as the 1920s gave way to the 1930s and the labor movement and the 1950s gave way to the 1960s civil rights movement, so it would be that the 1980s, a private-interest decade, would give way to the 1990s, a public-interest decade. I believed the political winds and tides were aligned for a decade of progressive change for America. I had been elected at just the right time to be a part of this change.

When President Clinton, in his first State of the Union speech, announced he would veto any health care legislation that did not provide universal coverage, that every citizen must be covered, I jumped to my feet and cheered. Finally, our country would have some form of national health insurance, and I would help make this happen. This was why I came to Washington, to make this kind of change.

There was reason to be optimistic. Democrats were in the majority in the House and the Senate, and the president made it clear that comprehensive health care reform was his top priority. I told Howard Metzenbaum, who was sitting next to me during the president's speech, "The Republicans will have a tough time being against this. We have a new president who will lead the fight and people want this change. They want more health security for their families. We can win this fight." I had *no idea* what a fight it would be.

My first hint came at an informal meeting with Democratic senators who were interested in health care. Whenever the Senate takes up a major issue, the leaders of the two parties gather together senators with expertise or strong interest. These working groups often become very important in developing policy and political strategy.

I spoke about my interest in a "single-payer" health care plan, similar to the Canadian system. Doctors and hospitals would remain in the private sector—this was not "nationalized" health care—but there would be one insurer or payer, like Medicare. Indeed this could be called "Medicare for all." The prestigious *New England Journal of Medicine* had devoted extensive coverage to this plan, pointing out that by eliminating the middleman role of the insurance industry, you would have huge cost savings, and provide comprehensive coverage for every citizen. Citizens would actually pay less in premiums for much better coverage. Indeed, both the General Accounting Office and Congressional Budget Office issued reports confirming the journal's analysis.

I had actually campaigned on this "single-payer" plan and was eager to introduce the legislation. It was a sobering discussion, especially when Ted Kennedy, *the* health care senator (whom I admire), said, "I agree this plan is the best proposal. But it does not have a chance. The insurance industry hates it, and it will go nowhere. It is just not realistic." He was drawing on *decades* of experience trying to pass comprehensive reform.

Ted was trying to be helpful, but I left the meeting completely disillusioned. I could not accept the proposition that a proposal that was the best policy and could truly help people, and that had not even been brought before the American people, could be "dead on arrival" because the insurance industry opposed it. This wasn't supposed to happen in a representative democracy! In Washington, "realistic" health care reform was already beginning to be defined by what was acceptable to the insurance industry.

With Jim McDermott, a congressman and physician from Washington, I introduced the "single-payer" plan, called the Health Security Act, in spite of the advice. First you start with the most desirable, I thought to myself, and it is only later on that you work out what is politically feasible. I refused to admit defeat before we had even begun to fight, and I was hoping that our legislation would pull the debate in a more progressive direction. Otherwise, too much of the energy and organizing and opposition to President Clinton's plan would come from the right. At every step along the way, as opposition grew, the plan would become weaker and weaker.

For a while, this strategy worked. Single-payer supporters in the Congress had access to the White House. This meant organizing discussions with health care policy advisers and meetings with Hillary Clinton, who was leading the charge. We generated some media coverage and participated in the national discussion and debate.

But soon the tide turned. The trillion-dollar health care industry, led by the insurance companies, went on the attack. The infamous "Harry and Louise" ads, pointing out the horrors of "government medicine," were but a part of it. The pharmaceutical industry and business community were united in their fierce opposition to health care reform. The National Federation of Independent Businesses (NFIB) was especially effective. Small businesses in every congressional district were armed with "information" about the danger of national health insurance. Intensive lobbying in Washington and, more important, in congressional districts made a difference—a big difference.

Media coverage shifted to accommodate this power. It was "horse race" coverage: which plan was ahead in Congress, which had the best chance of passing. There was precious little coverage of the strengths and weakness of the different proposals and what might be best for the American people, a failure, I think, of the media to be responsible. Citizens, armed with this critical information, could have then decided what they supported and informed their representatives and senators. By accepting the Washington definition of *realistic,* defined by a distorted pattern of power, the media denied citizens the opportunity to be empowered with knowledge and information and to make a difference.

The outcome might have been quite different if the American

people had received adequate information. In October 1993, soon after Bill Clinton described his health care plan on national television, the Jefferson Center sponsored a Citizens Jury on the topic. The Jefferson Center, founded by a wealthy, idealistic Minnesotan, Ned Crosby, believed that Citizens Juries were a way to democratize decision-making. A demographically representative group of people would hear different policy options, question experts, and decide the best policy.

Twenty-four jurors, broadly representative of the population (a slight majority had voted for George H. W. Bush for president), were brought together for five days in Washington. They were asked to address two questions: "Do we need health care reform in America?" and "Is the Clinton plan the way to get the health care reform we need?" Toby Moffett, a former congressman from Connecticut, and his witnesses spoke for Democrats, and Vin Weber, a former congressman from Minnesota, and his witnesses spoke for Republicans.

The single-payer option was excluded. Crosby had apparently decided to accept the Washington view in order to gain legitimacy. But he did invite me to drop by for a brief appearance on the jury's third day. Being from Minnesota, and given that we are friends, I think he felt guilty!

The jury was well into its deliberations, but I was allowed a short amount of time to make my case. I could read their faces and tell that they were genuinely interested in the single-payer plan. They voted right after the presentation to invite me back the next day so they could learn more. It was democracy in action.

By the fifth day, it was clear that many of the jurors were ready to change the ground rules and vote for the single-payer option. In the end, they backed away from this last-minute change and voted only on the original question. The emphatic vote was nineteen against the Clinton plan and five in favor.

Kathleen Hall Jamieson of the University of Pennsylvania's Annenberg School for Communication had been comoderator of the jury with Crosby. Off the record, she explored which plans the jurors preferred after being immersed in the health care debate. Seventeen out of twenty-four jurors raised their hand for the "Wellstone plan."

The Citizens Jury had not been let in on the secret that the single-payer plan was not to be considered seriously in Washington by legislators or the media.

Moreover, progressives or liberals who advocated "medicine for all" legislation were dysfunctional. We talked to ourselves. I spoke at many pro-single-payer gatherings around the country. I loved the people, especially the doctors (usually family practice doctors and pediatricians) and nurses who cared so much about their patients. But we never moved beyond a small family of fighters that, though right, never became much of a political force. Too many single-payer advocates assumed that proposing the correct solution to the problem would automatically set the legislative machinery into gear. They forgot the missing ingredient: *power*. We never organized a grassroots constituency powerful enough to successfully fight for the change.

The only way we could have beaten the health care industry would have been with dramatic and effective citizen politics. For example, we needed to organize a health care accountability day. On the same day, all across the country, there would have been face-to-face accountability sessions with representatives and senators.

Washington, D.C., was too expensive a trip for most people, so why not have meetings at home, organized by citizens pushing for health care reform? There is no substitute for face-to-face meetings. This is the epitome of representative democracy. And it is effective grassroots politics.

It would have been a big story in every single congressional district. It would have been a big story in each state. It would have been a big national story because the grassroots gatherings would have happened everywhere, on the same day at the same time. Representatives and senators would have had to participate because we go home all the time, especially during holidays and recesses, and there would have been no excuse for not meeting with constituents. This kind of bold citizen politics could win real health care reform.

It never happened. Progressives didn't organize effectively enough to really make the case. The White House, with the resources and a national forum and the power, also failed to galvanize the American people to fight for better health care. They tried to win with "inside politics"—that is to say, cutting deals (making compromises) with different economic interests to gain their support. The first part of the president's plan to go was cost containment, which was key to reform. Without the cost savings, where would the money come from for universal coverage and comprehensive benefits? But while the insurance industry and pharmaceutical industry had no problem with universal coverage, they were adamantly opposed to cost containment. More coverage meant more demand. Indeed, more demand would enable private interests to raise prices. Cost containment meant there would be accountability, and private interests would not have free rein to charge whatever they wanted. Appropriate profits were fine, but excessive profit off the sickness, illness, and misery of people would be challenged. The administration didn't have the political will to stand up to powerful interests and therefore never asked the American people to take on this fight.

With each accommodation of private power, the president's plan became more and more complicated. It reminded me of my book about farmers' struggles over a power line in west-central Minnesota. You never could understand how this high-voltage line became so crooked unless you realized it skipped a town or county here and there where powerful, well-connected people lived. The president's plan weaved and bobbed in the same way. Lee Lansing, who owns a hardware store in Northfield, put it best to me: "Paul, I might be for the Clinton plan if I understood it. But how can you be for something you don't understand?"

The motivating force for change would have to come from an energized, empowered public. Progressives understood this but didn't have the capacity to make it happen. The president and too many Democrats in Congress either didn't understand this or were too beholden to or frightened by the powerful health care industry to even try.

I have introduced the Health Security for All Americans Act in the Senate. Tammy Baldwin and Dave Obey have introduced it in the House. It is legislation worth fighting for.

Its first premise is that every American is entitled to have health care coverage as good as what members of Congress get.

Its second premise is that good health care must be affordable. Americans should not go broke trying to keep their bodies fixed. From my experience traveling around the country, I know that

Americans are willing to be responsible for an affordable, fair share of the cost of coverage and care. Under the Health Security for All Americans Act, a family's financial responsibility for health care would be based on a percentage of its income. At the lowest end of the income scale, families would be responsible for no more than 0.5 percent of their incomes. At the higher end of the scale, families would be responsible for no more than 7 percent of their incomes. For example, a family of four with an annual income of twenty-five thousand dollars would be responsible for no more than eleven dollars a month in total health care costs, while a family of four with fifty thousand dollars in annual income would have the security of knowing that its total out-of-pocket health care spending (premiums and cost sharing) could not exceed 5 percent of family income, or $2,500 per year.

The legislation's third premise is that citizens must have access to care when they need it. That is why it includes strong patient-protection provisions.

The act's fourth premise is that good health care delivery doesn't just happen. It depends on a well-trained, well-compensated health care workforce that doesn't have to worry constantly about where the next dollar is coming from. And I am referring to doctors and nurses and orderlies and home health workers and nursing-home workers—*all* health care workers. If we are going to deliver dignified, humane health care in this country to everyone, we need to start by treating the health care workforce with dignity and respect.

My experience has taught me that Americans agree with these premises, but they are not sure what the best way to act is. That is why the Health Security for All Americans Act is a federal-state partnership that says, "Here is what Americans want; you—the states—design the plan you want to get there, and we the federal government will provide the majority of the funds you need to reach that goal in the manner you choose."

States that submit plans early and achieve universal coverage would be rewarded with increased federal dollars for their efforts. But all states must have plans in place within four years and coverage for all their residents within five years. States could reach these goals in a variety of ways: with an employer mandate, with a combination of public and private initiatives, with single payer, or some other method. I think this is a good approach because it allows the states flexibility, but it clearly sets out a fair and just goal.

As we expand Medicare, we must expand flexibility. If states have their own designs for universal, affordable, comprehensive health care, then they should be able to use that instead. This legislation fits the mood in our country. It is decentralized public policy. We are a grassroots political culture, and it is best to let states pursue their own paths, consistent with our national goals. "The market" won't solve the health care crisis. But that doesn't mean the solution is big-government centralization. There will be and should be much more public support for this decentralized national health insurance proposal. Interestingly, the Robert Wood Johnson Foundation is considering this as one of several national health care proposals.

I've written this legislation in partnership with the Service Employees International Union (SEIU). I am excited by this joint proposal because the SEIU is a great, progressive union that is committed to "organizing the unorganized" and understands the importance of grassroots organizing to win this fight.

This proposal could cost seven hundred billion dollars over

ten years, only one third of the projected budget surplus. The money would be well spent. But Washington took the issue of universal coverage off the table. We need to put it back on. Back in 1993–1994, we had high unemployment, record deficits, and thirty-eight million people without health insurance. Yet we were debating comprehensive health care reform. Today, with record low unemployment, record budget surpluses, and forty-five million people without health care coverage, we are not even talking about it.

This time, we need to raise the issue in a way that can win. We must learn from the 1994 struggle. The first lesson is to have a proposal that fits the mood of the country and that people can understand. The second lesson is that you can't have major health care reform unless you build a movement to demand it. You need an empowered public to shout, "We want health security just like members of Congress have." When it comes to health care, if you don't have a real, galvanized citizen constituency to fight for the proposal, the people's interests don't have a prayer.

That America is the only major industrialized nation without guaranteed health care is a tribute to the power of the industries, investors, and heavy hitters that oppose it. The experience of the 1994 attempt to expand health coverage teaches that the potent insurance industry understood external politics well. They demonstrated their strength with an array of tactics ranging from their barrage of television advertisements starring "Harry" and "Louise" to their orchestrated targeting of individual senators and to their expensive, sophisticated lobbying campaigns.

We need to get people energized and involved. We need to motivate and coordinate progressive organizations. We will need active citizen politics to triumph over powerful money politics. Joan Samuelson's story is a perfect example of the power of active citizen politics.

Joan was only thirty-five, but she had Parkinson's disease. I was in my first year in the Senate when she testified before the Labor and Human Resources Committee. She pleaded for more National Institutes of Health (NIH) funding for research to find a cure. She described, in a very personal way, this devastating neurological disease.

Tears came to my eyes as she testified, as I thought of both her and my father. I don't know how many in that packed hearing room noticed, but Joan did. This was the beginning of a very strong bond and friendship.

At first, it was only Joan and a handful of others with Parkinson's who came to Washington. People were embarrassed by the disease—the uncontrollable shake, an inability to walk well, the difficulty (for some) of even speaking. But Joan was determined to change this. She, along with Ann Udall, the daughter of Congressman Mo Udall (who himself had severe Parkinson's), organized the Parkinson's Action Network (PAN). They were tired of the pity and charity. They were focused on advocacy for and by people struggling with Parkinson's disease. I joined them.

I introduced the Morris K. Udall Parkinson's Research Act, which required the NIH to dramatically increase research into the disease and to work closely with the Parkinson's community. My Senate cosponsors were Mark Hatfield from Oregon and, later, John McCain, who made it his business to visit Mo Udall regularly at the Veterans Administration Hospital in Washington.

I remember speaking at one of the early PAN meetings. About

thirty people were there, and I gave an intense speech about how we would grow in number and never give up until we found a cure for the disease. As I was leaving the meeting, a man stopped me. I was in a hurry, but he shook and held on to my hand so that I would not be able to rush by him (quite often older people will do this, too, because they are so used to us doing so). He said, "Senator Wellstone, I appreciate your speech. But speeches are not enough. Help us organize so we can have some power. I don't have that much time." He broke down crying. I knew he was right. Time was not on his side, and the Parkinson's community would have to raise Cain to get more research funding.

Joan Samuelson also knew this, and she was determined. A former lawyer, she found out that she had Parkinson's at age twenty-eight, one year after she had gotten married. My dad was sixty when he was diagnosed with Parkinson's. If the disease progresses slowly, then at least you've lived most of your life fully. But at age twenty-eight, the prognosis, no matter how you look at it, is grim.

Joan approaches her work with an understandable sense of urgency. PAN became a strong national organization, with thousands of members. It is now known as the Michael J. Fox Foundation, and Fox is using his celebrity in a courageous way to support political advocacy for people struggling with Parkinson's. Morton Kondracke, a respected journalist with many Washington connections, has added his powerful voice to this effort; his wife, Millie, struggles with the disease. And no one should forget Muhammad Ali and what he has done for this cause. Even with all the devastating symptoms, which have made him quite unlike the physical marvel he once was, Ali has bravely stepped forward to support the community.

One evening, I was fortunate enough to receive an award for my Senate work on Parkinson's. Ali and his wife, Lonnie, were to present the award. But it was 8:00 P.M., and he was obviously very tired. He had the blank look that appears sometimes on people with Parkinson's. So Lonnie presented me with the award. I kissed her on the cheek. All of a sudden, Ali's facial expression changed, and he raised his fists and stood over me. He had that wonderful twinkle in his eyes. This was a great moment in my life.

But even given the undeniable importance of celebrity support, PAN has taken off as a citizens' lobby. It may take people struggling with Parkinson's more time to get from appointment to appointment, but they come from all over the country to meet personally with senators and representatives, the NIH, and the media. Only people with the disease can argue the power of their cause in Washington and in meetings with elected officials in their states. They can exert real grassroots pressure on decision makers. And they have done so. Democrats and Republicans take this community very seriously. Best of all, the NIH now makes Parkinson's research a real priority.

Joan Samuelson and the Parkinson's community in Washington are perfect examples of a winning citizen politics. This is the way we can win health security for all Americans.

Chapter 3

—

A RADICALIZING
EXPERIENCE

My brother, Stephen, who is eight years older than I, was a straight-A student in high school. But I noticed as a kid that he didn't have any friends and seemed afraid of people. For my sixth birthday party, my mom was expecting ten kids to show up. She didn't know that I had invited the whole neighborhood—fifty kids showed up! With Stephen, it was different. I never remember him having any friends over to our house.

He went to Antioch College, and during his first year we received a phone call that changed our lives forever. Stephen had suffered a severe mental breakdown and was in a catatonic trance. My parents were devastated. I felt as if a dark gray cloud had moved into our house. For two years, the house always seemed dark to me—even when all the lights were on. It was such a sad home.

My brother was in a mental hospital for two years. The first year was at the Henry Phipps Psychiatric Clinic at Johns Hopkins, and the second at the Virginia State Mental Institution in Staunton. It took my parents twenty years to pay off the bill.

At first, I was afraid at Johns Hopkins. My brother looked and acted so different. His appearance and manner frightened me. He was very withdrawn. But the Phipps Clinic was a good place (though very expensive) by 1955 dark-age mental health standards.

I visited Stephen every Sunday and soon was comfortable enough to roam the "mental ward" and make lots of friends—that is the way it seemed to me as a kid. And my brother seemed to be getting a little better. Increasingly, he talked more with me.

My parents could not afford the Phipps Clinic, so eventually Stephen was transferred to the Virginia State Mental Institution in Staunton. It was a snake pit. Eleven years old, I visited Stephen every other weekend (Staunton was a long drive from our home in Arlington), and I came to hate that part of Virginia. The institution was a scary, depressing place: decrepit buildings, patients in institutional uniforms sitting on benches or wandering aimlessly. I didn't see how anyone could get better in that place.

I was more angry than frightened. I could not believe that vulnerable people who were sick, especially my own brother, could be treated so badly. These visits were a radicalizing experience. I didn't know what to do about it, but I knew this was an injustice.

It is interesting how we develop our philosophies. My sixth-grade class was outside during recess playing kickball, and an overweight boy was being ridiculed for being a bad player. I stopped the game and came to his defense with a passionate speech about Stephen. I told the kids that the reason Stephen became sick was because kids made fun of him when he was our age and that we should not make fun of anyone, that we should be nice to one another. I may not have had a full understanding of the causes of mental illness, but I was on to a good idea!

Stephen came home at age twenty. But his return home didn't end the darkness in our house.

There were many crises. Stephen was frightened that he would have to go back to a hospital again. He was afraid he could not survive on his own (though he did have extensive psychiatric outpatient care). His reaction to some of the drugs he was taking was truly terrifying. There would be many years of struggle.

The discrimination against those battling mental illness only added to Stephen's difficulties. When he reapplied to college at age twenty-one, the application included the question, "Do you have any history of mental illness?" He answered yes and was rejected by every school to which he applied. Stephen, remember, had been a straight-A student in high school. The next year, I think he finessed the question and was accepted to American University, from which he graduated in three years, Phi Beta Kappa.

I am very proud of my brother. His whole life has been a struggle, but he has survived and sometimes flourished. He was, before early retirement, a gifted fifth-grade teacher in Arlington, Virginia, with tremendous empathy for kids who didn't quite fit in. He now lives and works in Minnesota. I wish he could still teach; that was his passion. But he just can't do it. He lives on his own, however, and in the face of overwhelming odds, is able to be independent. I wish Stephen could have had a happier life with family and friends. I desperately want to see others who struggle with mental illness get better treatment.

A Trip to Tallulah

If we are to live up to Hubert Humphrey's "moral test of government" for "those who are in the dawn of their life, the children," then we must also turn our eyes to "those who are in the shadows of life, the sick, the needy, the handicapped." Today, throughout America, we are failing the moral test of how we treat the children who live in the shadows of mental illness. We have an obligation to see that these children get the help they need.

In 1842, Charles Dickens bemoaned the prisons and asylums he had found in America. Dickens said that he expected more from what he called the "Republic of My Imagination." Today, more than a century and a half later, I still expect more from the republic I imagine for America. And I am still reeling from my trip to Tallulah, Louisiana, in 1998.

One July day, I went with members of the National Mental Health Association to the Tallulah Correctional Center for Youth. I went because I had seen Justice Department reports of abuse of children in this facility; the vast majority had not committed any violent crimes, and some had not committed any crimes at all. I heard that there were kids who had just been dumped there, many with mental illness. And then, to make matters worse, they received little or no medical care, mental health or addiction treatment, counseling, or education. I was determined to use my position to expose these unconscionable conditions.

I was stunned. I saw a sea of black faces. I felt like I was in South Africa, pre–Nelson Mandela. I first met with Louisiana state officials in the administrative building. We had to have some initial negotiations because I wanted to visit the solitary confinement cells. I wanted to find out why kids were put in these cells for up to six or seven weeks at a time, up to twenty-three hours a day. They wanted me to visit the new cafeteria.

We first visited the cafeteria where these kids—kids between the ages of eleven and eighteen—were eating. There are five-hundred-plus kids in this facility. I went over to some of them and asked, "How are you doing?" And one kid said, "Not so good."

I said, "What do you mean?"

"This food," he replied, "they never serve this food. They just did this for today. We don't ever get this kind of food. These clothes, we never had these clothes. Every day it's the same clothes. Every day it's the same underwear. It's hot. There's no air-conditioning. These shoes, we never had shoes like these. Smell the paint on the table. These tables have all been freshly painted. This is just a show for you, Senator."

I turned to officials from Louisiana, and I never heard them contradict that.

Then we walked across the compound to the solitary confinement cells. Suddenly, one young man ran toward me and the crowd that was with me. I said to him, "You're going to get in a lot of trouble. Why are you doing this?"

"This is a show. And we're all going to get beaten up when you leave. We get beaten up all the time."

Then I met with four teens. One had stolen a moped, and two were there for breaking and entering. They also talked about being beaten up all the time.

One child was suffering from hallucinations and was being kept in isolation for observation, yet his transfer to an appropriate mental health facility was unscheduled and uncertain. Another child I met was taking three different types of powerful psychiatric medications but had seen a psychiatrist only twice in the previous eight months. The Justice Department report chronicled instances in which boys were being repeatedly sexually and physically abused, and children with mental illness were being housed with youths who had committed violent crimes—mentally ill children who had received no therapy. When these children exhibited the symptoms of their mental illness, they were often isolated or punished.

What is happening to these troubled children—dumped in these facilities without care—is a national tragedy. All across our country, more than one hundred thousand kids are detained in some type of jail or prison. These children are overwhelmingly poor, and a disproportionate number of them are children of color.

By the time many of these children are arrested and incarcerated, they have accumulated in their short lives long histories of problems. As many as two thirds suffer from mental or emotional disturbances. One in five has a serious disorder. Many have substance-abuse problems and learning disabilities, and most of them come from troubled homes.

Tallulah is not the only offending facility. The Justice Department has exposed gross abuses in Georgia and Kentucky and in other juvenile facilities. Investigators found extreme cases of physical abuse and neglected mental health needs. They found unwarranted and prolonged isolation of suicidal children, some of whom were also hog-tied. They found physical restraints used on youths with serious emotional disturbances. They found forced medication and denial of needed medication. They found children with extensive psychiatric histories who are prone to self-mutilation and who never saw a psychiatrist.

Our current system fails the mentally ill. The screening and treatment of mental and emotional disturbances at correctional facilities are inadequate or nonexistent. Mental illness typically is addressed through discipline, isolation, and restraint.

If a child had a broken leg, would any institution leave that leg unattended? Why then, in America, are we leaving children with mental health problems without appropriate attention from health professionals?

We know what works: treatment. But our current system favors punishment over treatment. For children, we know that family-focused, individualized treatment, delivered in a child's community, can improve that child's mental health and deter him or her from antisocial behavior. Integrating these mental health and substance-abuse services with schools and child agencies on a local level produces even greater success. Linked with community services, these treatment programs have been shown to reduce children's contact with the juvenile-justice system by 46 percent.

We can no longer ignore this tragedy. The Tallulah facility was a national disgrace, as are many other institutions like it. The wholesale neglect of adults and youth with emotional disturbances in our prisons must end. We, as a society, have the moral obligation to see that they get the help they need.

People should be held accountable when they commit brutal or heinous crimes. When three sixteen-year-olds beat up an eighty-five-year-old woman and leave her for dead, one cannot feel sorry for them. But anybody who believes that treatment like that in the Tallulah Correctional Center is the answer is way off base. What we will get from housing children in these kinds of brutal conditions are brutal children. It is in the self-interest of every family in America to offer treatment to those who will benefit from it.

The trip to Tallulah was hard. It is one thing to read a Justice Department report; it is another to see the conditions with your own eyes. When we held a press conference outside the facility after my visit, I almost passed out. In part, it was the extreme summer heat. But mainly it was emotional exhaustion. I could not believe that at the end of the twentieth century, entering a new millennium, such barbaric conditions could exist, that we could treat any child this way. My mind kept going back to Stephen and the Virginia State Mental Institution. Not much had changed in forty years.

The trip to Tallulah, I think, was some of the best work I've done as a senator. We exposed deplorable conditions. The media coverage was extensive. The New Orleans *Times-Picayune* wrote an editorial titled "Anarchy at Tallulah." It started out asking a question that pointed out the severity of the problem: "What was a senator from Minnesota doing at Tallulah?" The state, which had privatized the facility, soon took back control, the warden resigned, and Louisiana officials committed publicly to improving conditions at Tallulah. I am skeptical but can keep the pressure on from the Senate. And most important, the visit helped legitimate and validate the struggle of courageous people such as mental health advocates Mike Faenza and Shannon Robshan and activist lawyer David Utter, who, almost alone, had for years been trying to improve conditions at places like Tallulah.

As a direct result of that trip, I have proposed legislation that will provide funding for states to better assess and look for alternatives to incarceration for kids struggling with mental illness, for training juvenile-justice personnel to recognize kids struggling with mental illness, and for allowing juvenile-corrections facilities to have trained staff to provide treatment for mentally ill kids. Much of this legislation I've introduced as amendments to other bills, such as the Commerce, State, and Justice Department appropriations bills. The amendments have passed the Senate. The question is usually whether we can retain them in conference committees. (A brief political science lesson on conference committees: Rarely does a bill pass both the Senate and House in identical forms, in which case a conference committee comprising senior members from the Senate and House meets to iron out the differences. The conference committee is called the "Third House of the Congress," because critical decisions are made there, and the legislation is then reported to both the Senate and House for an up-or-down vote, without any opportunities for amendments. Conference committees, which have enormous power, are the least accountable to the public, and afford special interests many opportunities to influence legislation.) I will keep pressing. We have criminalized mental illness, and that is unconscionable.

An Unlikely Ally

Pete Domenici is an unlikely ally. Once, when I phoned his office and his personal assistant asked why I was calling, I answered, "Angela, it is about mental health, what the hell else do we agree on?"

Domenici is a conservative Republican, and we seldom vote on the same side of an issue, but Pete's daughter struggles with mental illness. He and his wife, Nancy, care deeply about this issue. I had learned this one night when I was asked to speak at a National Alliance for the Mentally Ill (NAMI) gathering in Washington, D.C. NAMI, a strong advocacy organization, was honoring Pete Domenici's work. It was the first time I spoke publicly about my brother, Stephen (with his permission).

Domenici and I, conservative Republican and liberal Democrat, realized we had a common bond, and we became committed to working together. We focused on ending discrimination in health care coverage. Our mental health parity legislation required that mental illness be treated like every other illness. All too often, insurance companies and managed care plans arbitrarily restrict coverage for the mentally ill.

Our strategy for change was threefold: a compelling message— *end this discrimination;* education showing that mental illness is a diagnosable and treatable disease; and grassroots organizing by citizens' groups to fight for the change.

The two of us formed a mental health working group that grew to include thirty-five senators. The best experts and thinkers in the country provided invaluable briefings for senators and staff. Most important, families that struggled with mental illness became active. They refused to accept the stigma and to be treated as second-class citizens. They were an empowered citizens' lobby, unified in their support of our legislation.

The business community and the insurance industry were adamantly opposed to this legislation, and that almost always means an initiative is dead on arrival. But the mental health community was not to be denied. There were face-to-face meetings with every senator, which made it hard for them to say no. The issue was no longer about statistics and abstract arguments but rather constituents who spoke personally about how mental illness affects their daily lives. They made compelling arguments, imploring their elected officials to end the discrimination against them so they could get treatment and have a chance to live decent lives. This kind of personal lobbying was effective. Senators were moved by what they heard, and it was hard for them to turn these citizen lobbyists down.

Not surprisingly, Domenici and I did not always agree on the timing or content of the legislation. I was the impatient one, pushing for the strongest legislation possible. Our debate was over what was realistic.

It was July, and it was time to act. The Kennedy-Kassebaum Health Insurance Protection Bill was the scheduled Senate business. This legislation prohibited insurance companies from limiting coverage for people because of preexisting illness or disability. It seemed like the perfect vehicle for our amendment.

But we were worried, and the stakes seemed so high. If we did not get a good vote (more than forty votes), then our cause could be set back years. We were in the Republican cloakroom trying to decide whether this was the time to "fight it out." Domenici turned to me and said, "In my gut, I think we should go." We did.

But for a variety of reasons there were only five minutes left in which to act, and there were other decisions and compromises to make. I wanted to include coverage for substance-abuse treatment. Domenici was emphatic: If we tried to cover substance abuse, the amendment would not pass. Moreover, he felt we could apply parity—the same treatment for mental illness as physical illness—only to lifetime and annual limits. In other words, insurance companies would no longer be able to say arbitrarily, "We will provide ten thousand dollars lifetime coverage or up to two thousand dollars for annual coverage, but that's all." Senator Domenici felt, however, that full parity covering hospital days, outpatient visits, co-payments, and deductible levels went too far. We didn't have the votes. We weren't even sure that we had the votes for a modest mental health amendment.

I hated this compromise. I felt we should be doing much more to end all the discrimination in coverage and that we left too many loopholes for the insurance industry with our incremental approach. But now we had only a minute left to make a final decision. In my heart, I knew Domenici was right. I respected his political judgment, and I knew our unity was essential to success. We left the cloakroom and came directly to the floor to introduce our amendment.

Those in opposition, like Senator Phil Gramm from Texas, argued their case: This was a government mandate, it would be hugely expensive, and health insurance premiums would skyrocket for everyone and price hardworking families out of coverage. This was an effective political argument, especially when combined with the political power of the insurance companies and business community.

But we were shaken when Ted Kennedy and Nancy Kassebaum announced their opposition, not on the merits but because they had decided to oppose all amendments to their legislation, to keep their bill "clean," with a better chance of passing Congress and being signed into law by the president. Indeed, these two highly respected senators were able to defeat all the other amendments to their legislation. But not this one. Something quite unexpected and extraordinary happened: Democrats and Republicans came to the floor without notes to speak in emotional, personal terms in support of the amendment. Senator Domenici spoke about his daughter, I spoke about my brother, Alan Simpson from Wyoming spoke movingly about his beautiful young niece who suffered from depression and took her life at age twenty, Kent Conrad from North Dakota spoke about his young assistant who also took her life. One personal, powerful speech followed another. Rarely have I seen such emotion on the Senate floor.

It was time to vote. In the Senate, we do not vote electronically. Each senator has to come before the Senate clerk and vote. This gives you a chance to talk with each senator personally before they vote. Domenici worked the Republican side, I worked the Democrats. Unexpectedly, senators came to me before I even had a chance to chase them down, and they said, "This is very personal and important to you, isn't it? I am going to support you." Domenici heard the same sentiments on the Republican side.

Once we were over fifty votes, other senators, who had voted against the amendment out of loyalty to Kennedy and Kassebaum, changed their votes to support the amendment. There were seventy votes in favor. Kennedy, a longtime champion of treatment for mental illness, looked relieved.

But the insurance industry is a formidable foe, and they managed to get the amendment knocked out in conference committee. The insurance industry defeated us, but not for long. I convinced Domenici we should attach the mental health parity amendment to Veterans Administration appropriations legislation. He did not like adding an amendment to an unrelated bill, especially an appropriations bill, but I was used to this kind of guerrilla warfare.

Domenici agreed to this tactic because it might be our last opportunity before adjournment. Also, he was angry. Over many years, this very formidable, conservative Republican senator had ably defended the interests of the business and insurance communities. Armed with data from independent studies showing the cost-effectiveness of our amendment, exposing the industry's "scare tactics," Domenici confronted his traditional allies: "To the business community opposing this amendment, I say: *shame on you, shame on you.*" This time, the debate was harsh and angry. But without Kennedy's and Kassebaum's opposition, we received even more votes—seventy-five. And this time we kept the amendment in conference committee, and it became the law of the land.

How this victory was won was as important as what was won. Men and women with mental disorders became their own leaders, their own advocates. It was their voices, their grassroots lobbying that made the difference, and they knew it. This legislative victory, the first in a very long time, empowered them. It built confidence and whetted their appetites for more. This was just the beginning for a determined citizens' group that would continue to press for more fairness and more justice.

What was won was significant, but this was only a first step. Only companies with more than fifty employees were covered— another compromise to head off intense small-business opposition. Also, if companies' health care expenditures rose by more than 1 percent annually as a result of this amendment, they would become exempt from the law. This was yet another compromise that I hated, but one that was entirely necessary to pass the amendment.

But we all knew there was more to come, and it was better to have a small victory—or big victory, depending on your point of view—than to be shut out. This was a community that did not need another defeat, and this was a community empowered to fight for more.

The next step is to pass the Mental Health Equitable Treatment Act. Too many health care plans severely limit the number of hospital days and patient visits for people struggling with mental illness. Copayment and deductible levels have risen for mental health treatment. This discrimination is unconscionable and results in people going without treatment or families going bankrupt. Sometimes, it results in death.

This was another bipartisan effort, but it took almost one year of negotiation. Bipartisanship is not all it is cracked up to be! I wanted full parity for mental illnesses; Domenici wanted full parity for what he describes as "serious mental illness"—certain specified diagnoses. The compromise: We expanded his list to include a broader range of mental illnesses and increased benefits for hospital days and outpatient visits. And all businesses with more than twenty-five employees would be covered, with no 1 percent cost loophole.

An impressive group of mental health citizens' groups are organizing to fight for this legislation. We have Democrats and Republicans as cosponsors. I believe we will pass it, but not without a tough fight.

My major disappointment is that I've never been able to convince Senator Domenici to include substance-abuse coverage. So I've had to go it almost alone in the Senate for several years. I've introduced the Fairness in Treatment Act, but it has little Republican support. Arlen Specter is the only one who has stepped forward to cosponsor this legislation. In spite of overwhelming evidence that addiction is a serious medical illness, we continue as a country to treat it as a moral failing. As a result, there is hardly any insurance coverage for people, and many go without any treatment.

Compared to mental illness legislation, it has been even more difficult to move substance-abuse-treatment parity legislation, which I have introduced. It is not because senators do not have any personal experience with this disease—it is pervasive in our society; we all know someone who struggles with alcohol or drug abuse. The missing ingredient is power. There is an important recovery community out there—undoubtedly some readers belong to it—and there are many success stories of people who, because of treatment, have turned their lives around. But unlike mental health, there is no voice, no empowered citizens' lobby, to fight for change. The Fairness in Treatment Act will languish unless we have a constituency to fight for it.

Jim Ramstad, a Republican congressman from Minnesota, is the lead sponsor of this legislation in the House. A recovering alcoholic, Jim speaks openly and honestly about his own personal struggle. But the recovery community must speak out, too. Recovering alcoholics and drug addicts cannot remain anonymous. They need to tell their powerful stories.

William Cope Moyers is a perfect example. He has told his story of cocaine addiction and of being in and out of treatment several times. He is today a wonderful husband and father, a powerful speaker, and an advocate for ending the discrimination against and providing substance-abuse treatment to people who need it. His father, the renowned journalist Bill Moyers, has produced a brilliant documentary, *Close to Home,* on addiction as a brain disorder. This education work is critically important. Science points to addiction as an illness, but public understanding lags way behind the data. There is little sympathy for addicts. Only when this disease hits home do people radically change their points of view.

Our challenge is to educate the public and organize the recovery community to be a political force for change. William Moyers and others are now doing this. As a senator, my focus is on good legislation—the Fairness in Treatment Act—*and* good organizing. Whenever, wherever people in the recovery community come together to build coalitions and become a political force, I try to be there to support their important political work. This is a vital struggle for justice.

Struggles for social justice take place throughout our country and on many issues. For example, Mary and Al Kluesner should be famous. The Kluesners started SA\VE—Suicide Awareness\Voices of Education—eleven years ago. They ran it out of their home for the first ten years. The membership is primarily people who have lost a loved one to suicide. The personal and mutual support is critically important. SA\VE also focuses on how to prevent suicide. The Kluesners, who lost two children to suicide, have somehow summoned the courage to help families all across America. They are supported by their surviving children in this effort.

I don't remember when the Kluesners and I first started working together. I do remember Sheila and I attended a SA\VE gathering about five years ago. We joke with the Kluesners about politics. Al and Mary are stalwart Republicans, but mental illnesses—depression, addiction, suicide—have no party affiliations. They are the third leading killer of young people between the ages of fifteen and twenty-five, and they strike families all across our country.

It is deeply troubling how little we as a nation do about suicide.

Where is the hue and cry? Why do we put so little value on these lives? As Kay Jamison, a brilliant psychiatrist, teacher, and author who has written so movingly about her own struggle with depression and attempted suicide, aptly puts it: "The gap between what we know and what we do is lethal."

My comprehensive suicide prevention bill is meant to help close this gap. The bill includes support for more basic and clinical research on mental illness and addiction; increased funding for community-based educational and prevention programs; support for the development of educational materials for families, health care professionals, and educators; and support for more funding for treatment.

One of my main priorities is, in fact, already included in the Children's Health Act of 2000. During negotiations about this bill, we fought hard to include a suicide prevention program for children and adolescents. It was an uphill battle, as this particular bill initially excluded any mental-health-related programs, a position that was completely unacceptable to me. We were ultimately successful in our efforts to include authorization for a seventy-five-million-dollar suicide prevention program. We made it very clear that any children's-health bill must recognize mental health as a major public-health issue, and must do more to prevent suicide among our children.

We have a full legislative agenda! I am optimistic. We have momentum. The books, articles, and documentaries are coming out. The media are more focused on mental illness. There is more of a focus on children who are struggling. Most important, there is an effective citizens' movement to fight for the change. The status quo is no longer and never was acceptable.

Chapter 4

IF WE ARE NOT

FOR OUR CHILDREN,

WHO ARE WE FOR?

When historians write about American politics over the past several decades, the ultimate indictment will be of the ways in which we have abandoned children and devalued the work of adults who take care of children.

Every politician wants to have his picture taken with a child—the smaller, the better. I've seen public officeholders deliberately position themselves next to children in front of the television cameras. Politicians especially love to have their pictures taken while reading to children. Campaign commercials show candidates surrounded by children. This is a winning political strategy.

Fannie Lou Hamer, a grassroots civil rights leader from Mississippi, used to say, "I'm sick and tired of being sick and tired." It is hard not to be sick and tired of the way too many politicians play photo-opportunity and symbolic politics with children's lives. We are all for children until it comes to digging in our pockets and making the necessary investment. But we will have no real national security until we are willing to invest in the health, skills, and character of our children. And this cannot be done on the cheap.

In the Beginning

One cannot begin too early to nurture a child's mind. About three weeks into a pregnancy, a thin layer of cells in the human embryo folds inward to form a fluid-filled cylinder called a "neural tube," where cells proliferate, a quarter million a minute, to bring together a child's brain. Even that early, a mother can affect her nascent child with the food she eats (or fails to eat), the drugs she takes, or the infections she incurs. A tiny slip in the intricate developmental process could result in a life of epilepsy, mental retardation, autism, or schizophrenia.

Adequate maternal nutrition and prenatal care provide the important first steps toward a child's mental development. The Special Supplemental Nutrition Program for Women, Infants, and Children (WIC) plays an important role, reaching seven and a half million people with nutrition assistance, counseling, and health referrals. The Clinton-Gore administration was right to expand participation by 30 percent. We need to ensure enough funding so that no expectant mother who needs help goes without it.

When a baby is born, its brain contains as many impulse-conducting cells, or neurons, as the Milky Way has stars. It starts with essentially as many nerve cells as it will ever have—the rough stone from which to chisel a lifetime of thought. Next, the baby's brain spins trillions more connections (synapses) between these neurons than it can possibly use. A young child's brain has twice as many synapses as its mom's or dad's. But over time the brain winnows away connections that it seldom or never uses. Neural activity, driven by the young child's sensory experiences, takes the baby's brain and progressively refines it into a child's mind.

Much depends upon the first three years of development. Early care has decisive, long-lasting impact on how children develop, their ability to learn, and their capacity to control their own emotions. The quality of child care can affect a child's language and cognitive development. But if we do not seize those opportunities, then the windows may begin to close. If children do not receive proper care before their third birthday, they may never have the chance to develop into fully functioning adults.

At the very least, why can't we fully fund the vital Head Start program for young children at risk, so that every eligible child can benefit? The Clinton-Gore administration deserves credit for working with Congress to increase Head Start funding by 68 percent. But even with those increases, only four out of ten eligible children get help from Head Start.

Seven in ten mothers now work outside the home. Ten million children thus need federal child care assistance, but the government provides subsidies for only 1.4 million of them. Fully 86 percent of eligible children spend their days unattended or in inadequate, often overcrowded facilities. The waiting lists for child care assistance in many states include tens of thousands of families. Children receiving inadequate care today will struggle in school and society tomorrow.

The National Council of La Raza reports that the child care problem is particularly acute among Hispanics. While two out of five white and African-American three-year-olds attend preschool, barely one in five Hispanic three-year-olds does. While nearly nine out of ten whites and African Americans finish high school, only six in ten Hispanic students do.

We must greatly increase child care funding. Many parents do not have the means to provide adequate care for their children. Parents who can barely afford rent cannot take advantage of the Family and Medical Leave Act and sacrifice weeks of pay to directly supervise a child themselves. Many mothers need to return to work shortly after giving birth and find that the only option open to them is to place their children in care that is substandard, even potentially dangerous—but it is the best care they can afford. There are not even enough child care slots for tens of thousands of mothers coming off welfare.

Care for one four-year-old costs an *average* of $4,940 in Columbus, Ohio, $4,990 in Atlanta, $5,070 in Raleigh, $5,200 in Kansas City, $6,140 in Seattle, and $7,900 in Boston. To meet these costs, families with incomes under $15,000 a year spend, on average, more than a quarter of their total income on child care. Parents can easily spend more in a year on quality child care than on public-college tuition.

Families making 85 percent of a state's median income are eligible to receive child care aid through the federal Child Care and Developmental Block Grant (CCDBG). Fully half of all American families with young children earn less than that, but only four states provide child assistance up to that level. In thirty-two states, a family of three earning twenty-five thousand dollars a year, about 85 percent above the poverty line, makes too much to qualify for help. In West Virginia, a family of three making more than fifteen thousand dollars no longer qualifies for child care aid. There is plainly not enough funding to support the huge need for child care assistance.

President Clinton was able to modestly expand care for children from poor families, though even this leaves fully 80 percent of eligible children without aid. Congress should pass legislation to put at least twenty billion dollars over five years into new funding for the Child Care Development Block Grant (CCDBG). And we should expand tax credits for low- and middle-income working parents, so they can better afford quality care.

We must improve the quality of child care in our country. Fully six out of seven child care facilities in this country provide only poor to mediocre service. One out of eight centers actually puts the safety of children at risk. To get their licenses, hairdressers and manicurists must receive 1,500 hours of training at an accredited school, but thirty-nine states and the District of Columbia do not require child care providers to receive any early-childhood training to care for children in their homes.

We should advance more public-private partnerships in which states and local businesses work together on the professional development of child care workers. We should offer greater loan forgiveness to those who earn a degree to work in early-childhood education.

And to attract and retain skilled child care providers, we need to raise the salaries we pay to those who care for children. Child care workers earn an average of only $11,780 a year and few receive benefits or paid leave; preschool teachers earn an average of $15,580 a year. Some teachers, recognizing the importance of preschool education, want to teach the very young but simply cannot afford to. It is a scandal that so many child care workers are working poor, without decent wages or health care coverage. It is no wonder that in any given year, there is a 40 percent turnover in staff. The children, of course, are the ones who pay the price.

Nine out of ten police chiefs agree that "America could sharply reduce crime if government invested more in programs to help children and youth get a good start" such as Head Start and child care. Mayors across the country identify child care, more than any other issue, as the most pressing issue facing children and families in their communities. And the people support it.

Our national goal must be to ensure that every child, by kindergarten, knows the alphabet; colors, shapes, and sizes; how to spell his or her name; and has been read to widely. We can achieve this goal. Tutors, mentors, and other volunteers at the community level can make real differences. But community volunteers are no substitute for the very best early-childhood development programs— not custodial ones—that nurture and develop the intellect and souls of our children. This will require well-paid professional teachers, assisted by skillful and well-paid teaching assistants.

An honest commitment to children means special attention to them in the critical early years of their lives. We need a national commitment equivalent to the efforts to build our vast network of federal highways, to the moon shot, or to the GI Bill—the very best developmental child care supported in every community in our country. The federal dollars would support community-based programs. This is where the federal government could be and should be a real player—investing money in prekindergarten education. To date, our response has been pathetic. The proposition that our country, with all its affluence, in a time of record economic performance, cannot afford to help children during these critical early years is unacceptable.

Twenty-first-century Public Education

Learning can ignite a spark in a child's life that, if gently shielded from the winds, can generate a lifetime of creativity and accomplishment. Extinguishing that spark is the cruelest and most shortsighted thing we can do. But in too many children, the spark of youth dies out.

I once went to Tunica, Mississippi, in the Delta. I had been to the Delta previously, retracing the steps of Bobby Kennedy. I went back because a marvelous teacher, Robert Hall, said at a community meeting, "I wish you could come back around graduation time, because only about fifty percent or just a little bit more of our students graduate, and our students need to have more hope."

A man picked me up at the airport and told me I would be addressing the third- and fourth-graders before visiting the high school. (In Tunica, the public high school is virtually all African-American, and the private schools are virtually all white.) Addressing the third- and fourth-graders on the last day of school didn't sound like a good idea to me. But I went to the elementary school, and I asked the third- and fourth-graders what they liked about school. A girl said, "I like it because a good education will help me be all I want to be in life." When I asked the students what they wanted to be, forty hands shot up at one time. They had all sorts of dreams; they had hope. The only problem is that for too many kids, this hope isn't there by the time they get to high school. I've tried to go to a school every two weeks. It's heartbreaking to meet an eight-year-old kid who doesn't really look at you and is completely beaten down.

I hosted a visit by a group of children from the South Bronx. Jonathan Kozol had written about these children's lives in his moving and powerful book *Amazing Grace: The Lives of Children and the Conscience of a Nation.* Jonathan, a very dear friend, thought they would be impressed by visiting a senator. I was certainly impressed with them. Even given their difficult lives of poverty, they were filled with imagination.

But then I started thinking of their future. "Of these thirty kids," I asked the adults with them, "how many will make it through high school?"

They smiled sadly. "Two or three," one responded.

The literary critic George Steiner once said that teachers have a special responsibility to build "echo chambers" inside children so that the great achievements of the past can resonate within them. Imagine if we could help all of America's children's dreams ring with the glory of a nation's great achievements. Imagine the opportunities.

Just when more than a million teachers are nearing retirement, the coming decade will see 11 percent more high school students. This demographic intersection—we need 2.2 million new teachers over the next ten years—provides a golden opportunity to inspire, train, and hire a new generation of bright young teachers and send them into the public schools fresh with ideas and new energy. But this nation cannot buy golden opportunities with tin-cup funding. We need to champion the vision of an Education Century.

Some counsel that the problem is too large or too complex for societal response. They are wrong. We know what we need to do. We may not know all the answers, but we know enough of them that we have no excuse not to act. Too many focus on the difficulty of the problem merely as a means of evading responsibility.

We need to make sure that students come to school prepared to learn. That means we must address the prenatal care and child care needs discussed above.

We need to start in the early grades to enhance children's self-esteem and to foster their interest in school and learning. By investing in these preventive efforts up front, we can avert violence, drug abuse, and pregnancy during adolescence, improving school performance and saving money.

We need to reduce class size. As laudable as the Clinton-Gore administration's efforts have been in bringing one hundred thousand new teachers into the system by 2005, we need so many more new teachers simply to meet current demand. We know what works. Reducing class sizes in the early grades to fifteen to eighteen students improves student achievement; we should commit the funds to make it happen.

We need to rebuild our crumbling school buildings. I have asked senators during a floor debate how well they would do if we had no air-conditioning during the hot Washington summers, if the heating was inadequate during the winters, if the toilets didn't work, if the copy and fax machines were broken, if there was no e-mail, if the roof leaked during rainstorms, if the building was decrepit, rather than majestic. "These are the conditions facing millions of schoolchildren," I shouted out on the floor of the Senate. "What kind of message do we send these children? We are telling them that we don't value or care about them."

We need to fund education sufficiently so that teachers' salaries are high enough to attract the very best. I've visited hundreds of high schools as a senator, and in every discussion about education, the students always emphasize the importance of good teachers. I ask, "What makes for a good teacher?" They say, "Someone who gets to know and cares about us; someone who respects our views and encourages discussion; someone who makes the subject interesting and important to our lives; someone who challenges us to think on our own and doesn't just have us memorize and answer worksheet tests."

I typically ask, "How many of you are interested in becoming public-school teachers?" Rarely do more than 10 percent answer yes. They cite low salaries and lack of respect. I turn to the teachers and ask them in front of the students, "You have heard what the students have said. Why do you teach?" When they reply—and their responses are almost always about the reward that comes from teaching, encouraging, and helping students and about making a positive difference in their lives—students listen intently. It is very moving. They *do* value their teachers, especially the teachers who add so much to their lives.

We should develop criteria for children that draw on their interests and strengths. Children who live in inner cities can learn just as much as children who live in the suburbs, if schools can structure lessons that connect to their lives. Colin Greer, president of the New World Foundation, notes how he frequently sees children in inner-city New York who have mastered concepts of physics and statistics, at least as they apply to baseball. Greer asks, Why can't schools in their curriculum take advantage of these kids' knowledge and experience? In addition to physics and mathematics, students could, through studying baseball, learn about geography, history, ethnic studies, and more.

We need to implement bold strategies to increase parental involvement in our schools. Nine out of ten children who get A's and B's have parents who participate in their education. And few variables correlate more directly with the educational success of students than the economic and educational background of their parents. We should expand the role of schools as the educator of the community, not just the children. As Greer proposes, schools should draw parents in by offering adult-education programs about things such as English proficiency, job skills, job hunting, and the fundamentals of democratic citizenship.

We must do more to provide funding to less affluent school districts. More correlation exists than people may want to acknowledge between the resources devoted to education and the outcomes that result. Adequate funding is a necessary, if not sufficient, condition for success, for making sure that every child has an equal opportunity to learn. Jonathan Kozol writes in his book *Savage Inequalities:*

> A 14-year-old girl with short black curly hair says this: "Every year in February we are told to read the same old speech of Martin Luther King. We read it every year. 'I have a dream . . .' It does begin to seem—what is the word?" She hesitates and then she finds the word: "perfunctory."
>
> I ask her what she means.
>
> "We have a school in East St. Louis named for Dr. King," she

says. "The school is full of sewer water and the doors are locked with chains. Every student in that school is black. It's like a terrible joke on history."

It startles me to hear her words, but I am startled even more to think how seldom any press reporter has noted the irony of naming segregated schools for Martin Luther King. Children reach the heart of these hypocrisies much quicker than the grown-ups and the experts do.

One can do no better than to quote Kozol's conclusion:

All our children ought to be allowed a stake in the enormous richness of America. Whether they were born to poor white Appalachians or to wealthy Texans, to poor black people in the Bronx or to rich people in Manhattan or Winnetka, they are all quite wonderful and innocent when they are small. We soil them needlessly.

It is incredible that children in our country must go to schools without enough textbooks, without proper heat, without adequate lab facilities, in dilapidated buildings. Usually, they simply do not have the financing. They do not have the best teachers or even computers. Huge disparities exist.

Sometimes lawsuits have been the only way to bring about change. One came out of Hartford in the early 1990s, contesting the enormous disparity in per-pupil expenditures between neighboring districts. Although Connecticut had the highest per-capita income in the United States, Hartford was the fourth-poorest U.S. city, with the second-highest rate of poverty among children. At the same time, not surprisingly, the Hartford school system had substantially inferior educational resources than other school systems. Hartford students were shortchanged on many educational fronts. For example, school systems across the state spent an average of $147.68 per student per year on textbooks and instructional supplies; in Hartford, it was $77, only 52 percent of the statewide average. Hartford school enrollment, incidentally, was more than 92 percent minority, whereas nearby towns such as Avon, East Granby, and Wethersfield were less than 5 percent minority.

Or consider East St. Louis, Illinois, in the late 1990s. Students in East St. Louis faced backed-up sewers that flooded school kitchens, faulty boilers and electrical systems, regular student evacuations and canceled classes, dangerous structural flaws, exposed asbestos, malfunctioning fire alarms, emergency exits chained shut, instructor shortages that usually meant students did not know in advance whether they even had a teacher, and school libraries that were typically locked or destroyed by fire. Needless to say, these students (and too many others) had little access to technology.

How can we expect our children to achieve when they face this? How can they learn to develop? How can they realize any—let alone all—of their potential in such an outrageous environment?

I went to a meeting with school principals from Minneapolis and St. Paul to talk about the needs of their children. We agreed, first, that we need to address the learning gap. Too few of our children have the reading skills necessary to succeed. It is painful that so many children come to kindergarten way behind in very basic skills. Quite often, they then fall further behind and end up dropping out of school.

But the talk quickly turned to something else—it became a discussion about mental health. A lot of their children find it difficult to learn because they have serious personal, emotional struggles. They have seen their mothers beaten, or they have been beaten themselves. They see violence everywhere.

I have done a lot of work with Vietnam veterans suffering from post-traumatic stress disorder. That's essentially what many of these kids are suffering from.

Washington Post columnist William Raspberry recounts the story told by Kenneth Dodge, director of Duke University's new Child Policy Center:

> Dodge uses the allegory of a man who's placed himself at the bottom of a waterfall, working feverishly to rescue children as they plummet over the cascade. "He hauls them out, nurses their wounds, takes them to the hospital—and begs for more money to continue and expand his rescue work. He's a hero."
>
> He's a smart hero, though, and it dawns on him that if he could get up to the top of the fall, he might be able to keep a lot of kids out of the dangerous waters in the first place. The problem: More youngsters will fall while he's climbing the cliff. And so he stays where he is.
>
> That, says Dodge . . . is what happens with troubled children—particularly poor children—in American society. We "treat" (with suspensions, expulsions, detentions and incarcerations) those children who fall into antisocial and violent behavior. But the behavior so disturbs us that we don't dare walk away from it, even if we're convinced we could do more long-range good at the prevention end.

There is so much that needs to be done for these children. We need community-based efforts to provide supportive services for children at risk. We need to get some real mental health help for these children to pull them out of the stream before they drop over the waterfall. We should fund training for mental health professionals, probation personnel, detention officers, lawyers, and juvenile-justice service providers to help them identify which troubled children could advantageously be diverted from detention and incarceration into community-based programs. Except in the very short run, diversion is cost-effective, and it is also the right thing to do. Investing in services to divert troubled children now makes so much more sense than investing in jails to house them later.

We need to provide hope to young children that there are high schools and colleges in their futures. We should foster mentoring partnerships with high schools and colleges so that eight-year-olds and ten-year-olds know that there are rewards for them if they study and work hard.

And you can see the results when you visit a school that works well. The teachers have training. They are free to teach; they're not straitjacketed by resource constraints. Both teachers and administrators have high standards. They expect the children to do well. Every child knows that she or he is loved—every child. The kids are full of hope. They have plans for their future. We can get it right.

Holding Kids Responsible for Our Failures

We can also get it wrong. "High-stakes testing," touted as the new education reform, is a very harsh agenda for America's children, one that holds children responsible for our failure to invest in their future and in their achievement.

If there is any question about whether or not we have, as a nation, overemphasized standardized testing, and if there is any question that this overemphasis has taken so much of the excitement out of teaching and learning for so many people, a recent article in the Baton Rouge *Advocate* puts those questions to rest. Louisiana is in the process of implementing high-stakes tests, called LEAP. This article addresses how schools and students near Baton Rouge are dealing with the preparation and stress. The test, which lasts five days, will determine, among other things, whether students will be promoted and whether schools will face sanctions for poor performance.

The article describes one teacher who said, "I'm thinking about letting us have a scream day sometime in March, when we just go outside and scream." The article continues, "Her principal is keenly aware of the stress on both students and teachers. He told teachers during a meeting ... that he expects some students to throw up during the test. He's arranged to have all of the school's janitors on duty to clean up the messes." It is no wonder that students are anxious. According to the article, "For the past eight weeks, Northwestern's school billboard has been updated daily with the number of school days left until the test."

When I read this story, I wondered why we cannot let children be children. Why do we impose this misplaced pressure on those as young as eight? Making students accountable for test scores works well on a bumper sticker, and it allows many politicians to look good by saying that they will not tolerate failure. But it represents a hollow promise. Far from improving education, high-stakes testing marks a wrongheaded retreat from fairness, accuracy, and quality.

This is ironic, because standardized tests evolved as a way to ensure more equal opportunity in education. When used correctly, they are critical for diagnosing inequality and for identifying where improvement is needed. They enable us to measure achievement across groups of students so that we can make states and districts accountable for improving the achievement of all students. However, they are not a panacea. The abuse of tests for high-stakes purposes has subverted the benefits tests can bring. Using a single standardized test as the sole determinant for graduation, promotion, tracking, and ability grouping is not fair and has not fostered greater equality or opportunity for students.

First and foremost, it is grossly unfair to hold back a student on the basis of a standardized test if that student did not have the opportunity to learn the material covered on the test. It is absurd to suggest that students who attend the poorest schools have anywhere close to the same preparation and readiness as students who attend the wealthiest schools. People talk about using tests to motivate students to do well and to ensure that we close the achievement gap. But we cannot close the achievement gap until we close the gap in investments between poor and rich schools. We know what these key investments are: quality teaching, parental involvement, and early childhood education, to name just a few.

But when we impose high-stakes tests on an educational system where there are, as Jonathan Kozol says, savage inequalities, and then we do nothing to address the underlying causes of those inequalities, we set children up to fail. Instead of doing what we know will work, and instead of taking responsibility as policy makers to improve students' lives, we place the responsibility squarely on the students. This is simply negligent.

We must afford children equal opportunities to learn, but that is not enough. Even if all children had the opportunity to learn the material covered by the test, we still cannot close our eyes to the hard evidence that a single standardized test is not valid or reliable as the sole determinant in high-stakes decisions about students.

The 1999 National Research Council report *High Stakes* concludes that "no single test score can be considered a definitive measure of a student's knowledge" and that "an educational decision that will have a major impact on a test taker should not be made solely or automatically on the basis of a single test score." The 1999 edition of *Standards for Educational and Psychological Testing*, which has served as the standard for test developers and users for decades, asserts that "in educational settings, a decision or a characterization that will have a major impact on a student should not be made on the basis of a single test score." Even test publishers, including Harcourt, CTB/McGraw-Hill, Riverside Publishing, and ETS, consistently warn against this practice. For example, Riverside Publishing asserts (in *The Interpretive Guide for School Administrators* for the Iowa Test of Basic Skills), "Many of the common misuses [of standardized tests] stem from depending on a single test score to make a decision about a student or class of students." CTB/McGraw-Hill writes, "A variety of tests, or multiple measures, is necessary to tell educators what students know and can do. . . . The multiple measures approach to assessment is the keystone to valid, reliable, fair information about student achievement."

Politicians and policy makers who continue to push for high-stakes tests and educators who continue to use them in the face of this knowledge have closed their eyes to clearly set professional and scientific standards. They demand responsibility and high standards of students and schools while they themselves defy the most basic standards of the education profession. It would be irresponsible for a parent or a teacher to use a product on children in a way that the manufacturer says is unsafe. Why do we then honor and declare "accountable" policy makers and politicians who use tests on children in a way that the test manufacturers have said is effectively unsafe?

There is no doubt that when mistakes are made, the consequences are devastating. Study after study shows that holding children back leads to poorer academic performance, higher dropout rates, increased behavioral problems, low self-esteem, and higher rates of criminal activity and suicide. Research indicates that students who do not graduate are more likely to be unemployed or hold positions with little or no career advancement, to earn lower wages, and to be on public assistance.

Still worse, the effects of high-stakes testing go beyond their impact on individual students to their influence on the educational process in general. As research shows, such tests have had a deadening effect on learning. Studies indicate that public testing encourages teachers and administrators to focus instruction on test content, test format, and test preparation. Teachers tend to overemphasize the basic skills and underemphasize problem-solving and complex-thinking skills that are not well assessed on standardized tests. Further, they generally neglect content areas that are not covered, such as science, social studies, and the arts.

For example, the Consortium on Chicago School Research concluded that "Chicago's regular year and summer school curricula were so closely geared to the Iowa test that it was impossible to distinguish real subject matter mastery from mastery of skills and knowledge useful for passing this particular test." These findings are backed up by a recent poll in Texas that showed that only 27 percent of teachers there felt that increased test scores reflected increased learning and higher-quality teaching. Eighty-five percent of teachers said that they neglected subjects not covered by the state exam.

Around the country, teachers and students are under such pressure to perform that schools are actually using some of their limited funds to pay private companies to coach students and teachers on test-taking strategies. According to the San Jose *Mercury News,* schools in East Palo Alto, which is one of the poorest districts in California, paid Kaplan ten thousand dollars apiece to consult with them on test-taking strategies. According to the same article, "Schools across California are spending thousands to buy computer programs, hire consultants, and purchase workbooks and materials. They're redesigning spelling tests and math lessons, all in an effort to help students become better test-takers." The teacher from Baton Rouge I mentioned before had even bought blank score sheets with bubbles on them so students could practice filling in circles, as they have to on standardized tests.

The richness and exploration we want our children to experience is being sucked out of our schools. I was moved by an op-ed article I read recently in *The New York Times* that had been written by a fifth-grade teacher who obviously had great passion for his work. He said, "But as I teach from day to day . . . I no longer see the students in the way I once did—certainly not in the same exuberant light as when I first started teaching five years ago. Where once they were 'challenging' or 'marginal' students, I am now beginning to see 'liabilities.' Where once there was a student of 'limited promise,' there is now an inescapable deficit that all available efforts will only nominally affect." Children are measured by their score, not their potential, not their diverse talents, not the depth of their knowledge, and not their character.

We must never stop demanding that children do their best. We must never stop holding schools accountable. Measures of students' performance can include standardized tests, but only along with other measures of achievement, more substantive education reforms, and a much fuller, sustained investment in schools.

The battle has already begun. Two senators, a Democrat and a Republican, recently introduced legislation that would have mandated an "end to social promotion" in a clumsy and grossly unfair way. In response, I introduced an amendment that would have modified their amendment by saying that their remedy would not apply to any child who had not had proper early-childhood education, had not had access to Title 1 programs or to special-ed and bilingual education for which they were eligible, or had not been taught by fully qualified teachers.

The debate here was quite instructive. One of the senators said that the fully qualified teacher requirement was a "deal breaker" because in the senator's state there were far too many uncertified, underqualified teachers. Well, no one could have made my point better. That amendment and the system of high-stakes tests get the sequence backward. They lose sight of our fundamental objective: to provide children with the tools they need to achieve, to think critically, and to understand material deeply.

Truth, beauty, and justice did not prevail, and my amendment failed. I was, however, able to defeat the underlying amendment to end social promotion, which everyone had thought would pass. I was taking my usual several hours to make my point (the Senate is supposed to be the world's greatest deliberative body!) when Slade Gorton, a conservative Republican from Washington State who had been presiding during the debate, came up to me and said, "I am not going to support your opportunity-to-learn amendment, *but* I am not sure I like the idea of the federal government telling the states and school districts what to do about promotion." I thought to myself, "Wait a minute, I know how to win!"

Before the final vote on the social-promotion amendment, I made my case: "I have argued that there must be the same opportunity to learn for all children. You do not have to agree. I've argued that there is not a shred of evidence that holding children back, as young as age eight, helps them. It often hurts them. You do not have to agree. But consider this: This underlying amendment says that if your state chooses, in its wisdom, not to rely on standardized tests and hold kids back, the federal government will cut federal funds. For this reason alone, *you* [I looked at all the Republicans] should not vote for this." I got sixty-five votes, the majority of them Republicans. As they came up to vote, some of them said, "Very clever, Paul. You, as the states-rights advocate!"

As a senator, I am absolutely committed to the fight to stop the abuse of high-stakes tests. When the Elementary and Secondary Education Act reauthorization comes to the floor of the Senate, I will introduce an amendment that will require that states and school districts use multiple measures of student performance if they are going to use tests as part of a high-stakes decision. The amendment will also require that if tests are used, they must be valid and reliable for the purposes for which they are used; must measure what the student was taught; and must provide appropriate accommodations for students with limited English proficiency and disabilities.

I don't think this kind of amendment has much of a chance. It will be condemned as a "mandate." The federal government has no business telling states what to do or not to do, opponents will say. And at least one senator will remind me of my states-rights argument!

Sometimes the goal is to give people legislation to rally behind, to nurture and promote grassroots organizing. As it turns out, parents and students are sharply challenging high-stakes testing. They don't trust the reliability of a single test, and they don't like the drilling involved in studying for them. Their children hate it. School systems like that in Chicago, where this bandwagon started, are now, in the face of opposition, pulling back from relying on a single standardized test.

I am personally committed to this cause. According to standardized test scores, I was not supposed to even graduate from the University of North Carolina. Then, when I took the Graduate Record Exam, I received horribly low scores in English and math. The political science department was going to deny my admission to its graduate school. Since I could not afford to move, and since the department had such an excellent graduate program, I made a determined stand. I demanded to see the chair of the department. When his secretary said he was too busy to see me, I staged a single-person sit-in. I said I wouldn't leave without seeing him.

So we met. I told the chair that I made almost all A's as a political-science major and that I didn't see how he could say, on the basis of one standardized test, that I was not qualified. He eventually agreed.

I wouldn't have been able to pass many of the tests that are given to kids today. But this fight is not just about tests, it's about ensuring that all our children are educated well. It is time for us to promise equal opportunity for every child in America. To paraphrase Rabbi Hillel, if we are not for our children, then who will be? If we do not do right for our kids, then who are we? And if not now, when?

Chapter 5

—

. . . AND
ECONOMIC JUSTICE
FOR ALL

Our political philosophies are formed by our personal experiences. One of the reasons I believe so strongly in economic justice is that I've worked and organized with people for whom such justice is a seemingly unattainable dream. My work with the rural poor in Rice County, Minnesota, nearly cost me my job, but we were able to empower a group of working-poor mothers to move a step closer to equity.

For four years, I helped build a community-organizing group, the Organization for a Better Rice County (OBRC). I wrote about this experience in a book titled *How the Rural Poor Got Power: Narrative of a Grassroots Organizer.* My favorite chapter was titled "New Community Leaders" because that is what good community organizing is all about. The new fact of political life for Rice County was that people who had been viewed for years as "poor white trash" had become leaders. They were men and women who came to see themselves in a different light—as individuals of worth and dignity and substance. They became their own leaders. They, for the first time in their lives, spoke at county commission, school board, and city council meetings. They spoke out for themselves and their children—for decent jobs, for health care, for food assistance, for affordable housing, for adequate welfare. Most important, they changed public policy for the better, making positive changes in policy.

It was dramatic to observe and be a part of this. I rarely spoke at the meetings these new leaders attended. My goal was to encourage people to speak for themselves. There were many victories won *by* rural poor people. The OBRC grew in power. No longer were poor people invisible, powerless, and without voices. As important as what the victories did for people was what they did *to* people. I don't know that I've ever been more thrilled than to see a young woman speak for the very first time at a school board meeting—speak on behalf of her children—and to know that I had something to do with helping to build her confidence and make her a leader.

Many of these new community leaders also became my teachers. I learned firsthand about the grinding poverty of their lives and about their constant struggles to survive. I learned that rural poverty, while more hidden than urban poverty, was no less real. And most important, I met men and women who, in the face of difficult circumstances, managed not only to survive but to flourish— as parents and grandparents and citizen activists with the courage to challenge power and effect social change. They were grassroots heroes. And there is no doubt in my mind that none of the real changes would have occurred without this community organizing.

This experience has guided my work to this day. Of the one hundred members of the U.S. Senate, I suspect I am one of the few who has actually worked with a welfare mother, sat in her living room, spoken with her at gatherings, and strategized with her on issues. My work in Rice County later informed one of the most difficult political decisions I've had to make.

The Welfare Debate

Some of my friends and trusted political advisers (several are former students) came to our home. It was June 1996, and they were concerned about the welfare vote. President Clinton, who had campaigned on the slogan "Changing welfare as we know it," was calling this legislation "welfare reform," claiming it would replace welfare with work and economic self-sufficiency. The polls showed 80 percent support for this (not an unimportant fact for Clinton and many other Democrats).

We had a careful discussion. Some warned me that if I voted against the bill, I would lose my reelection campaign and be unable to fulfill other progressive initiatives.

I wish I could write that I jumped up and gave a rousing speech about preferring to lose an election on the basis of what I believed rather than winning on the basis of decisions I didn't support. Instead, I tried to weigh both sides. Myles Horton, founder of the Highlander Folk School and one of our country's great radicals (he was a central figure in both the labor movement of the 1930s and the civil rights movement of the 1960s), once told me a fascinating story. He and some coal miners were meeting with their senator from Tennessee, the great progressive Estes Kefauver. They insisted he support a strong labor bill. He listened and then said, "I'll vote for this, but I want you to know that it is my honest judgment as a politician that if I support this I won't be reelected. If I am not re-elected I can't do many of the things I can do for you. But if you want me to vote this way I'll do so. So given what I just said to you, tell me what you want me to do." Myles said they all told him to vote against the labor bill!

The reason welfare "reform" had become such a volatile issue, and the reason that a vote against the welfare bill was so difficult politically, was not that Americans are mean-spirited. People didn't really know about the specifics of the legislation. But welfare was a values question. People believed that if you valued work, you were for welfare reform; if you were opposed to reform, then you didn't really value hard work and economic independence. It was a false dichotomy, but this was a politically impossible point to make.

I made no decision during our meeting. But over the next few days I came to know in my heart that I would adamantly oppose this legislation. I remember thinking to myself, "If I were teaching my politics of race, gender, and poverty seminar, what would I be saying about this bill?" I knew I would be condemning it. More children would likely be plunged into poverty; the cut in food-stamp benefits was unconscionable; and this bill turned the clock back half a century, with the federal government no longer guaranteeing at least a minimal floor beneath which no poor, dependent child would fall. States would now be in control, and in all too many states welfare policies would be harsh.

Moreover, this was personal. I had organized with welfare mothers. I knew them and their children. I rejected the stereotypes and scapegoating that fueled "welfare reform"—namely, that welfare mothers were lazy and must be forced into work. The cuts in benefits to *legal* immigrants also hit home, given my immigrant heritage. I couldn't vote against my own roots. That's the way I saw it. I would be defiant.

During the debate, I was probably the most visible senator in opposition to "welfare reform." I railed for hours that I wouldn't vote for legislation that impoverished more women and children. But the angry words of one senator were no substitute for power, and we had precious little of it on our side.

At one point during the debate, Daniel Patrick Moynihan, the one acknowledged expert on welfare policy in the Senate, asked where the people were who would be hurt by this legislation. He was dismayed that there was so little organized opposition. Moynihan looked toward the front of the Capitol and asked why there were not thousands of protestors lined up all the way to the Supreme Court.

Moynihan had become so discouraged over this that he stopped coming to the Democratic caucus lunch on Tuesdays. Quite often, he was not on the floor during the debate, though he was the official leader of the opposition. He was bitterly angry with President Clinton and other Democrats for supporting a policy that was in his view cruel and callous and undid part of his life's work. I admire Pat Moynihan but wish he hadn't been so disheartened and had fought even harder. As it was, there were only a few of us, none with Pat's prestige and standing.

Without effective grassroots organizing and some real political

clout, there was no stopping this legislation. At the Democratic caucus meeting right before the final vote, Bob Kerrey, then chair of
the DSCC, said, "Paul, it seems like almost everyone is for this bill.
Why don't you summarize your position against it?" I told Bob, "I
am not sure you will like it. My position makes your job more
difficult because it is so politically unpopular." I went on to argue
my case against the welfare bill. Democratic senators were very re-
spectful, but I knew it would be a landslide vote, and it was, 89–11.
Interestingly enough, Kerrey, a Congressional Medal of Honor winner who was severely injured in the Vietnam War, voted against it.
I later asked him why, and he said, "When I think of all the government assistance I received after Vietnam, I am a supporter of providing government help to people who need it."

The political attack back home was fast and furious. I was the
only senator up for reelection who voted against the bill, and the
Republicans were ready to make this a key issue. In an unexpected
way, however, there was a lot of personal support from the opposite
side, from Republican senators who congratulated me on voting
my convictions.

Then there were the late-night calls from the Clinton administration. Labor secretary Bob Reich was sympathetic. One of the
nicest and most surprising calls came from Leon Panetta, the president's chief of staff, who was very complimentary and gracious.

President Clinton and his successor have since proclaimed welfare reform a huge success, citing a 50 percent reduction in the case
rolls. But what about reducing poverty? That is the key question.
Where are the seven million women and children no longer on welfare? What kinds of jobs do the mothers have? Are they living-wage
jobs? Do the families still have health care coverage? (Medicaid cov-

erage came with AFDC, which had been gutted.) Most important, what kind of child care is available? Are the children safe?

I once traveled to East Los Angeles and visited a wonderful Head Start program. After spending time with the children, I sat down to talk with the parents. One mother told me that she had been on welfare but was now working. She emphasized how much she wanted to work. All of a sudden, she broke down and started crying because while she wanted to work, she was frightened every day for her little girl, who was a second grader. She was scared because she was no longer there to take her daughter to and from school. She had instructed her little girl that, once home (in the housing project) each afternoon, she was to take no phone calls and not go outside. How many children cannot go outside to play?

We do not know what will happen when state by state all women and children are cut off from welfare assistance. Will there be jobs for children who had children or have not graduated from high school, mothers who struggle with substance abuse, mothers with severely disabled children, or women who have been battered over and over again? If they can't work, these families will receive no assistance.

There is already some disturbing evidence: that 670,000 fewer children have health care coverage because of "welfare reform"; that there has been a sharp decline in food-stamp participation— the major safety-net nutrition program for poor children; that there has been a significant increase in the number of children living in the poorest households (where income is less than one half the poverty level); and that most of the jobs being obtained are low-wage and leave the families in poverty.

But so far I have not even been able to pass legislation requiring the Department of Health and Human Services to collect relevant data from states and report it to Congress. We, as policy makers, must insist on this. The first time I proposed this, I lost by one vote, 50–49. The second time, the Senate accepted this amendment (the Democrats said to the Republicans, "Do you want him on the floor for several hours on this?"), but then it was dropped in conference committee. The third time, I attached the welfare amendment to an education tax-credit bill. It passed 78–21. But the bill may go nowhere because it provides public money for private education. I need to look for another piece of legislation to which to attach this amendment.

I am determined to force an honest policy evaluation of the welfare bill. The health and well-being of poor women and children is literally at stake. Gunnar Myrdal, the Swedish sociologist, once wrote that "ignorance is never random." Democrats and Republicans ought to care enough to at least want to know.

Making Work Pay

The welfare controversy has diverted attention away from the real issue: reducing poverty in our country. After all, the majority of poor people in America are not on welfare: Of the thirty-three million poor people in America, eight million are welfare recipients. For the working poor, the discussion about welfare has little relevance. What good is welfare reform if we aren't willing to engage in a national debate about reducing poverty?

Welfare reform is a popular political issue because Americans value work and believe that people *should* work. But that does not mean that Americans support simply cutting off assistance and leaving people to the mercies of the job market. I learned from talking to Minnesotans that the same 75 percent of people who are in favor of welfare reform agree that if people play by the rules and work hard forty hours a week, almost fifty-two weeks a year, they should not be poor. The Pew Research Center also found recently that 74 percent of Americans feel that the federal government has a responsibility to end domestic poverty.

Our focus should shift to ending poverty. We should redouble our efforts to better the educational opportunities of the poor, through programs such as Title 1 and Pell grants. We should protect and expand the earned-income tax credit, that vital support of low-income working families, which President Reagan called "the best anti-poverty, the best pro-family, the best job creation measure to come out of Congress."

We should strengthen and more vigorously enforce laws that will ensure that people get equal pay for equal work. If employers simply paid all workers as much as they do men for any given job, the average working woman's family would earn $4,205 more a year. If states simply enforced equal-pay laws, it would cut poverty among single working mothers in half, from 25.3 percent to 12.6 percent.

And we should raise the real value of the minimum wage closer to its 1968 level. Right now, living on minimum wage means living in poverty and being stretched to the limit. David of Southfork, Pennsylvania, told a 1996 minimum-wage forum:

My wife Jennifer [and I] . . . need to work in staggered shifts so that we can take care of our two babies. One of the most difficult aspects of our work schedules is that we have very little time to spend together as a family. Our only real family time together is for three hours on Friday afternoons; an hour and a half on Saturday afternoons [and] Sundays, but only until three-thirty. . . .

Living on minimum wage means living with fear. At this same forum, Antonio from Texas said:

[We live] in our one-bedroom apartment in a high-crime area. So I work almost sixteen hours a day just to make ends meet. And I worry about my family alone in our apartment at night. I call them every hour at night just to make sure they're safe.

Living on minimum wage can mean living without a home of your own, as people who wrote to the Health, Education, Labor, and Pension Committee testified. Tonya from North Carolina said, "I stay at my parents' house with my uncle and my sister. I can't afford a place for me and my children. I tried living on my own but I had to go back home. . . . Everything is just so hard." And Mary C. of Albuquerque wrote: "I am a single mother with a toddler. The reason I am a single mother is due to domestic abuse. While I am a capable person, within the past six months because of the low minimum wage and the changes made in the welfare system, I have been homeless. Any changes in the minimum wage could only help people in my situation."

Living on minimum wage can mean going to soup kitchens and food charities. Food banks have found that two out of five client families have at least one person with a job. Among the people who came to the Neighbor to Neighbor food-distribution center in the basement of Christ Church in Greenwich, Connecticut, a *New York*

Times reporter found a cook from a local French restaurant, a construction worker, housekeepers from nearby estates, and a woman who cared for the children of housekeepers.

It is long past time to raise the minimum wage to a livable wage. Making work pay, combined with providing affordable child care and health care, would dramatically raise family incomes. These policies are vitally important to working families. Moreover, they are absolutely consistent with the values Americans hold dear about work, children, and families.

The Impetus for Change

Among the twenty-six leading industrialized nations, America ranks sixteenth in living standards among the poorest one fifth of children, seventeenth in rates of low-birth-weight births, eighteenth in income disparities between rich and poor children, and dead last in protecting children against gun violence. We face a burgeoning problem. Every thirty-six seconds in America, a baby is born into poverty; every forty-seven seconds, a baby is born without health insurance; every minute, a baby is born to a teen mother; every two minutes, a baby is born at a low birth weight; every three minutes, a baby is born to a mother who received late or no prenatal care; and every eighteen minutes, a baby dies.

The question is where the impetus for change will come from, because poor people are virtually invisible to the U.S. Senate. When I was teaching about Congress in my class on American politics, I emphasized the background characteristics of U.S. senators. They are disproportionately wealthy and represent, economically, only a narrow slice of the population. This, combined with the fact that the constituents that they see as most relevant, those in the best position to affect their tenures in office, are also disproportionately wealthy, leads to a serious imbalance of power. Too few people have too much wealth, power, and access, and too many people have too little.

I now realize that it is a far more serious problem—and a more distorted pattern of power—than I ever imagined. It always angers me how some senators who represent states with many poor people rarely mention poverty, much less try to do anything about it. Mississippi's Trent Lott, the Senate majority leader, is an example. Just think of what he could do in the positive to address poverty, so evident in Mississippi. But it is not his priority. Moreover, there are all his puzzling votes against housing, health care, and child care assistance for low- and moderate-income people. Why?

When I visited the school in Tunica, Mississippi, I got some insight about this. Some in the African-American community with whom I met told me that the majority leader had not visited and met with their kids, and that normally on his visits to Tunica he met only with the casino owners, condominium developers, and other wealthy white people. In other words, they may have technically been part of his constituency, but they certainly weren't part of his *political* constituency.

Or take Texas. Maine and Vermont recently signed a compact with Texas for disposal of "low-level" nuclear waste. Congress had to approve the compact. The problem is that the Texas state government had decided, in its wisdom, to locate the disposal site in Sierra Blanca, a poor Hispanic community that sits in, of all places, earthquake territory! There are communities that are more suitable, but powerful and important people live there. This was a classic case study of environmental injustice. The path of least political resistance was to target a poor "minority" community that couldn't fight back.

But the community did fight back. They asked me and the really gifted congressman Lloyd Daggett (from Austin) to help. There wasn't much that Daggett could do in the House of Representatives, though, because of some restrictions in House rules. It was "wiped" in the House. But in the Senate, I refused to accept any time agreement on debate over the compact and was able to hold it up for nearly two years. In the David vs. Goliath fight that ensued, Texas, Maine, and Vermont all hired lobbying firms, the utility companies were as always well represented, the governors pressed hard, and the vast majority of senators felt they had no stake—indeed, if *their* states were involved in a similar compact, they would want to count on the support of other senators. On the other side were a priest and a small group of citizens who could afford to come to the nation's capital by bus only once a year. As a result of my delays, however, we were able to organize more in Texas, and community people won this fight. In the face of intense citizen opposition, Texas found it difficult to justify a below-ground nuclear-waste dump site on a "geologically unstable formation." Texas had to move the site.

I managed to infuriate some senators. I was told that this was none of my business. My response was that if I had to vote on it, it was my business. I was warned that none of my own legislation would be approved if I continued the fight. But what troubled me was that low-income Hispanics were not on many other senators' radar screens. It was painfully clear that they didn't know these people and, most important, didn't feel any need to know them. They were not a relevant constituency.

I refuse to believe that I cannot make a difference on issues of economic justice. Only one hundred people get to speak on the Senate floor and have the opportunity to fight for what they believe in or, as is quite often the case for me, fight against what they don't believe in. I take full advantage of this honor. Quite often, I am trying to stop the worst: blocking cuts in low-income energy assistance; providing some protection for public-housing tenants; saving the TRIO program, which expands the participation of low-income students and students of color in higher education. Sometimes I am aiming for small victories, such as forcing a USDA study of hunger and declining food-stamp participation; or getting more Pell grant assistance for older, nontraditional community-college students; or allocating additional funding for Head Start. Sometimes I am trying to make the Senate focus on poverty, regardless of the legislation at hand. Since there is no germaneness rule in the Senate, you can easily change the subject in any debate. I consistently bring to the Senate floor amendments that deal with poor children, trying to add them to the Postal and Treasury, Interior, and Defense authorization or appropriations bills, to use but three examples. It is my way of ensuring that the U.S. Senate will address this issue. Sometimes I win, often I lose.

It can be very discouraging. Fighting hard, causing trouble, while absolutely necessary, is no substitute for positive change. That is why I am continually trying to use my position to validate and legitimate organizing among low- and moderate-income people. I am most excited about organized labor's commitment, under the leadership of John Sweeney, head of the AFL-CIO, to "organize the unorganized" (also the battle cry of the industrial unions in the 1930s). The organizing victory by the Service Employees International Union (SEIU) for seventy thousand home health care workers in Los Angeles in June 1999 represents, I think, the future. Sweeney has helped energize the labor movement. Andy Stern, president of SEIU, has led the way. *Fifty percent* of his union's budget is committed to organizing.

I try to visit low-income communities—in Mississippi, Appalachia, East Los Angeles, Chicago, East Baltimore, and urban and rural communities in Minnesota—in which people are struggling and are not used to seeing a senator. It is a way to legitimate their struggles for better lives. It is a way to nurture and support community organizing for progressive change.

Sometimes, these visits are very painful. One especially difficult one was in North Minneapolis, a low-income African-American neighborhood, where eleven-year-old Kevin Brewer had died. One night in 2000, Kevin had been alone at Cottage Park at 10:00 P.M. His mother, Tanisha, twenty-six, was working. His aunt was taking care of him, but Kevin was used to being on his own. Twenty men were playing dice near the park. There was an argument, and suddenly a series of shots rang out. Kevin, who was watching the argument, was shot in the chest. He died in the grass. He shouldn't have been there. He should have been at home, supervised by an adult. But the drug dealers and gangs shouldn't be there either, destroying the neighborhood and killing innocent children.

There is a memorial for Kevin at the spot where he was killed.

There are flowers and many notes from other children. One note reads, "Kevin, I'm sorry this happened to you. I hope you are in heaven."

There is trash on the sidewalks and street, drug dealers and gang members are everywhere, and decent families are terrified to go outside. Little children cannot safely play on the swings in the park.

Spike Moss, a community leader, and the Reverend Jerry McAfee are out every night with neighborhood volunteers to stop the drug sales and force the drug dealers out. It is a sidewalk-by-sidewalk, block-by-block fight. They need help from the police, to be sure, but, they ask, what happened to all the youth-outreach programs that were once available? Where are the job opportunities, the affordable housing, the positive futures for these kids to see?

Spike thanked me for coming when others wouldn't and said that by drawing attention to this area and its problems I gave him one more week's worth of volunteers. I was happy to help where I could, but I don't understand how it can be that no one has ever stepped forward with information about who killed this boy. I cannot accept these conditions in this neighborhood (and many other neighborhoods) that led to Kevin's death. I wish I could do more.

I've introduced legislation that speaks to many of these problems. But just proposing good solutions to problems does not assure that the machinery of government automatically gets into gear, especially in this Congress. The missing ingredient is power. Poor people like Kevin Brewer are invisible in America today. Senators may give speeches about the need for welfare reform, but the truth is that most spend very little time in poor communities. Most are not knowledgeable about these communities—even as they make decisions that crucially affect the quality of poor people's lives. Other children like Kevin will continue to be invisible, unless poor people organize and speak for themselves.

I want to end this chapter with a poignant case. In the midst of our booming economy, there is an economic convulsion going on in agriculture, and many family farmers are being driven off their lands. These families are in tremendous economic and personal pain. No matter how hard they work, they fall further and further into debt. They are losing their farms (typically fourth-generation farms), where they work and live, and which are all they have known. Some will take their own lives. Right now in rural America there is a severe strain on mental health services because of the threat of suicide. If this continues, we will lose an entire generation of producers.

The demise of family farmers is not inevitable. It is not the result of Adam Smith's invisible hand or some inexorable economic law of gravity that dictates that family farmers must fail. Rather, it is the result of a stacked deck: Huge agricultural subsidies have been given in inverse relationship to need, with most of the money flowing to large agribusiness, and the government has failed to take antitrust action against conglomerates that make record profits while family farmers go under. The farm-retail spread, the difference between what farmers make and the price charged consumers, is growing wider and wider, which benefits only the corporate middlemen. Livestock producers, for example, receive record low prices while IBP Foods, Cargill, ConAgra, and other packers make record profits. This is in part the result of a cruel and failed policy embodied in the Freedom to Farm Act, signed into law by President Clinton in 1996. In the name of deregulation, this legislation eliminated any chance for family farmers to get a decent price in the marketplace.

The general public has little patience for agricultural subsidies and for good reason. Over the four years since the passage of the Freedom to Farm Act (I and others call it Freedom to Fail), Congress has given thirty billion dollars to farmers, most of it to the largest producers, who are the least in need.

We should instead be enhancing the bargaining power of family farmers so they can get decent prices and support their families. This assistance must be targeted to producers who own and live on the land they farm, not on huge, absentee investors.

We should also focus on putting free enterprise back into the food industry. Right now, wherever farmers turn—who they buy their materials from, who they sell their grain or livestock to—they are faced with a few conglomerates that control well over 50 percent of the market. If antitrust action were taken and real competition were promoted, it would help family farmers to survive and even flourish.

President Clinton has told farmers that more exports will be their salvation. But the interests of exporters such as Cargill (the largest corporation in Minnesota) and those of family farmers are quite different. Exports mean nothing to producers if they cannot even get a price that covers their costs of production.

Add to this picture the alliances of grain companies, packers, and big chemical companies like Monsanto, and it is pretty scary. Food is a very precious commodity. And industrialized agriculture, with a few conglomerates controlling all phases of the production, just as oil companies do, is a food-security concern. These companies can charge any prices they want, and their bottom lines care little for the environment. The excessive use of chemicals and the huge animal-factory operations damage our land and water and do not provide safe food for our families.

The point is this: The health and vitality of rural communities is based not on the number of acres farmed or the number of animals owned but rather on the number of family farmers who live in the community, buy in the community, and contribute to and care about the community.

The problem is that family farmers are out of sight and out of mind for most Americans. The American people know little of this struggle and how it affects their lives. Rural America has to speak for itself. Farmers, in the words of the great 1890s populist orator Mary Elizabeth Lease, will have to "raise less corn and more hell."

I am emotional about all the pain I've seen—so many broken lives, broken dreams, broken families. I am on fire to change this. But introducing great legislation won't matter unless there is a galvanized constituency to fight for it. My role as a senator is to travel, speak, and organize, to call on farmers and rural communities to take a stand. I have traveled to Texas, Missouri, Illinois, Wisconsin, the Dakotas, and Iowa to organize farmers.

I went to one gathering of eight hundred pork producers at the stockyards in Sioux Falls, South Dakota, in the dead of winter. While I was speaking, I felt like I was speaking to a gathering in 1900. Here were these farmers facing destruction at the same time that a few packers were in hog heaven. It's the same issue: producers versus conglomerates. These producers—grain, livestock, and dairy farmers—are the last free-enterprise entrepreneurs in the food industry. Yet whether it's who they buy from or who they sell to, they are confronted with monopoly power. One demand that unifies family farmers is the demand for antitrust action. The interesting question is why the two major political parties aren't doing anything about it. Surely it is not coincidence that the firms that have monopoly power are the ones who can make the biggest contributions to elected officials.

While I was speaking to the pork producers, I was thinking one other thing, and I wondered if I should say it, given how much they were struggling and what a difficult time it was for them. But I went ahead, saying, "I want you to know that I am more committed to this than any other senator" (although South Dakota is represented by two superb senators, Tom Daschle and Tim Johnson).

They looked at me and must have thought, "What a conceited little guy."

But I said, "Let me explain why. My mother, Minche Danishevsky, is up there in heaven, smiling down at us, saying, 'Paul, good Jewish boy that you are—what are you doing with all those pork producers?' "

There was a roar of laughter. Even at a time of great hardship, they were able to smile and keep their sense of humor. At the risk of boasting, I believe I care more about the plight of the pork farmer than any other Jew in the Senate!

We need to raise the roof in Washington. We will bring thousands of rural citizens to the Congress. There will be tough face-to-face meetings with senators and representatives. There will be dramatic marches and rallies and other powerful direct action. And rural Americans will all report back to their communities when they return home whether their senators and representatives made a commitment to write a new farm bill that supports family farmers, not the large conglomerates that have muscled their way to the dinner table.

It is easier to write this than to make it happen. But I've seen up close whom Congress responds to and who is left out. We will never reorder the policy and priorities unless we reorder the power. And if we don't act soon, it will be too late; too many family farmers will be wiped out.

John Sundvor is a very fine journalist who writes for many of Minnesota's rural newspapers. He wrote that this is too unequal a fight, that family farmers and rural people don't have a chance against the powerful corporations that control Congress. He wrote that I am, with good intentions, raising expectations that will only be dashed later.

I worry that he will be proved right. But as I told John, there is no other choice but to try. We will never know what can be accomplished unless we try.

Quentin Burdick was a wonderful populist senator from North Dakota. I was lucky enough to know him before he passed away at age eighty-four. One Friday afternoon, Quentin observed me rushing out of my office to catch a plane to Minnesota.

"Where are you going?" he asked. I told him. He smiled and said, "Have a good trip home, but remember, you must always fight for the people." This was not rhetoric. He truly believed this. He was right.

Chapter 6

—

"EMBARRASSINGLY
LIBERAL"

We won the 1990 Senate race by asking people to vote for what they believed in. That proposition connected with Democrats—and many Republicans—who were looking for more than the politics of polls and conventional wisdom. Our win demonstrated that a politics of conviction can be a winning politics. The 1996 race would test that idea and be a referendum on the kind of citizen politics that we embodied.

I knew all along that it would be a tough race. I was the only senator up for reelection who voted against the "welfare reform" bill, and this vote alone was supposed to cost me the election. I was at odds with most of the powerful economic interests in the country, including in Minnesota. My friend Harry Reid, senator from

Nevada, told me, "Paul, you are the most difficult senator to raise money for!"

And Minnesota was far from an automatic win for Democrats. Republicans had won all the U.S. Senate races in Minnesota since 1978, and a Republican had been elected governor in 1990 and 1994.

The Republican Party in Minnesota began its campaign against me in 1993, three full years before my term was up! My outspoken positions on issues and my efforts to fight the Republican agenda (especially the post-1994 Gingrich agenda) made me the top Republican target in 1996. The Minnesota Republicans, using a particularly vicious attack-politics mentality, set a low standard that would eventually cost them.

In May 1994 at the Republican state convention, delegates were given brochures titled "Wellstone Watch," in which unflattering caricatures of me—with a big nose, short legs, potbelly, even in a dress—accompanied wildly untrue allegations and personal attacks.

This was just the beginning. The Minnesota Republicans also began to hold weekly news conferences, attacking me and distorting my statements and votes. Often, they didn't even bother sticking to any issues. A typical press release, from the spring of 1994, led with, "Paul Wellstone is a lying, hypocritical whiner." The Republicans also decided to follow me and my family with a video camera and tape recorder, hoping to gather incriminating statements that they could use in attack ads. At every public appearance, every speech, the Republicans were there, getting it all on tape.

The Republicans knew that my greatest political asset was the trust I had built with Minnesotans. Whether they agreed with me on all the issues, they knew where I stood, and believed I was committed to public service. The Republicans figured that the only way to defeat me was to raise questions about my trustworthiness. The problem was, the Republicans simply couldn't make this case without lying and making outlandish allegations. Minnesotans would see right through it.

While the Republican Party continued to attempt a smear campaign, Rudy Boschwitz prepared to run again for the Senate seat that he felt was his. Boschwitz, who seemed to be filled with resentment that he had been defeated by a underfunded, unknown, liberal college professor, was prepared to wage an ugly, negative campaign to defeat me. He hired the notorious political consultant Arthur Finkelstein, famous for his scorched-earth, win-at-all-costs negative campaigns, whose trademark was sticking opposing political candidates with the worst of all political labels: "liberal."

Not coincidentally, Finkelstein was also hired by the National Republican Senatorial Committee (NRSC) and its chairman, Alfonse D'Amato, to wage a soft-money attack against me. The NRSC started its ads early—in May, six *long* months before the election. These were "issue advocacy" ads. That meant they could bash me, with no limits on the amount of money spent on them or on how the money for them had been raised, as long as the ad never asked you to vote for or against me. Here was a typical ad: There was a picture of a prison guard tower, then one of a female stabbing victim lying on the ground; my picture was then "morphed" with this picture and joined by the words, "Paul Wellstone voted to let violent criminals out of prison." This ad was so outrageous that CNN journalist Brooks Jackson did a blistering commentary on it.

Meanwhile, Finkelstein's client Rudy Boschwitz began waging a campaign accusing me of being "embarrassingly liberal." At every press conference, in every ad, on every billboard, in nearly every sentence, the Boschwitz campaign returned to the same refrain: "Paul Wellstone is embarrassingly liberal." Billboards were put up with my picture next to the words, "Paul Welfare: Embarrassingly Liberal." This strategy had worked for Finkelstein before: Smear your opponent early and often. This line of attack didn't bother me.

I remember saying to Sheila early one morning as I was trying to anticipate what we would have to deal with that I was proud of the way I have lived my life. I had nothing to hide. But that presupposed that the truth mattered, and it didn't to this crowd. They would launch any attack that would work—as well as attacks that wouldn't.

What weighed on my mind the most was my family. I am enough of a fighter that attacks on me make me even more determined. But personal attacks that can hurt your family, charges that aren't true, are very frightening. I wondered, sometimes, whether this was worth it. I told Sheila that this would be my last campaign, that we would never have to go through this again. That is how I felt then. The larger point, of course, is that very few people will want to run for office if they believe it will be destructive for their family.

My indignation crested on the day that I first knew we would win.

It was early fall. Months of constant Republican "issue advocacy" ads, which we had not responded to (if we had spent money in the summer, we would have been broke in the fall), had had some effect. The race was very close, showing Boschwitz and me neck and neck at the end of the summer.

Sheila was back in Minnesota, campaigning, and I had had dinner with a close friend. Walking back from dinner through a park, she talked to me about a very painful and personal experience. We sat down together on a bench, and I listened carefully, at one point putting my arm around her.

I told Sheila about this the next day. She said, "I'm really touched by what happened. I just hope the Republicans didn't have their camera." My friend, it turns out, had spent the night worrying about the same thing.

As I listened to them, I thought to myself, "I am not going to let these people define me." They had created a climate of fear for people I loved, and I became determined that they would not win the election.

The Republican attack ads were fast and furious and went on and on. In mid-October they put on an ad showing a caricature of me speaking to a gathering of burned-out, dope-smoking, 1960s-style hippies—again with the tag line "Paul Wellstone, embarrassingly liberal." Some Minnesota journalists thought it was funny. One even wrote an article about how clever the Boschwitz campaign was in using humor as a weapon.

Minnesotans didn't agree. They had seen enough. The attacks had gone on for too long. This ad triggered widespread anger toward the Boschwitz campaign. Minnesotans thought associating me with drugs was vicious and untrue. Moreover, this kind of caricature of the 1960s is very insulting to many men and women who are very proud of their political activism then and what they were able to accomplish.

The Republican attack was most furious on the Iron Range, in northern Minnesota. Television ads are inexpensive on the Duluth stations, and Iron Range residents were barraged daily with attack ads that focused on environmental land-use issues that had led to the defeat of many Democrats over the years.

The most explosive issue was the Boundary Waters Canoe Area Wilderness (BWCAW). Rod Grams, Minnesota's Republican senator, was pushing, along with the area's Democratic congressman, Jim Oberstar, to restore "motorized" portages between the lakes in the BWCAW (a motorized portage allows a person to transport a boat with a truck). The issue heated up. Citizen organizations sprang up that demanded that more lakes be open to motorized boats and vehicles.

I believe that this is the crown-jewel wilderness area in our country, and so I was opposed to these proposals. The political problem was that part of my base—including steelworkers and the men and women who worked in the iron-ore mines—could turn against me. In the past, they had voted against environmentalist candidates.

The Republicans were only too pleased to fan the flames. Their ads attacked me as an "extreme environmentalist" who sided with liberals instead of with northern Minnesotans. I thought I could lose much support over this issue. When I spoke to the Minnesota AFL-CIO convention in the fall of 1996, I was worried about what the reaction would be. It turned out to be electrifying—the workers were on my side. I had been a strong labor senator, and at every word in my speech they were on their feet, cheering.

When I finished the speech, one of the most emotional I've given, I looked toward the steelworkers from the Range. I told them, "You have to win this for me. I'm counting on you to stand up to this attack. I need your support." I walked straight from the podium to where they were seated. I cannot describe the emotion and personal support I felt from them.

And they did help win the race for me. At work in the mines and with neighbors in Iron Range communities, they put in good words for me. Every time I campaigned on the Range, I was surrounded by a massive show of steelworkers. They organized everywhere I went. They literally lifted me on their shoulders to victory.

After we won, the next morning Sheila and I drove straight up to the Iron Range to thank people for their support. The conventional political wisdom is that a liberal Democrat can do well in the Twin Cities but not on the Iron Range, where positions on gun control and environmental issues can defeat you. But politics is personal. I think that more important than positions I had taken on labor and other bread-and-butter economic issues was the time Sheila and I had spent on the Iron Range, in communities with people: in cafés, schools, hospitals, child-care centers, senior centers, union halls, veteran halls, and small businesses. The Range was our second home, we were family, and all the political and personal attacks in the world could not break this bond.

———

How did we win? Why did we win? Minnesotans rejected poison politics. That was a critical factor. But there is more to the story.

The 1996 race was a textbook labor-intensive, grassroots campaign. Unfortunately, there is very little interest among political operatives in this kind of campaigning. I know from personal experience. The DSCC makes you feel guilty if you don't raise hundreds of thousands of dollars for Democratic senators up for reelection each cycle. They argue, "We all have to chip in if we are to regain the majority." I don't blame them for this pitch; it's their job. But when I offer to set up a field operation that can register and turn out the vote, the words fall on deaf ears. They still prefer to focus on who can raise millions and millions of dollars to get on TV with ads.

We built an incredible field operation in Minnesota. Between November 1994 and November 1996, we held eight hundred house meetings in Minnesota. Sheila and I attended many of them. Anywhere from twenty-five to two hundred people attended each. We raised money, discussed issues, and talked strategy. Most important, supporters *owned* the campaign in their neighborhoods and communities. Everyone left the meetings feeling good about their roles in the campaign. We kept it fun.

What we did was campaign statewide as if we were in a city-council race. I wanted our campaign to be decentralized and connected to the people.

We traveled again in the old green bus, reinforcing the grassroots nature of our campaign, with lots of hand shaking and stump speaking. We invested heavily in a smart and aggressive advance operation. Every stop was well planned and well executed, and we took our campaign straight to where voters lived and worked.

When the Republicans launched their last round of attack ads in the closing week of the campaign, we were ready. Our juggernaut was our organization, built block by block, town by town, over two years. In the final week, our campaign made, from early morning to about 10:00 P.M., *ten thousand* get-out-the-vote calls every hour, all made by volunteers! Our supporters went door-to-door in their communities, talking to their neighbors. (Who would you believe, an attack ad or your neighbor?) Barely 50 percent of the American people voted in 1996, a presidential election year. In Minnesota, we had a 65 percent turnout!

I was especially proud of the turnout in low-income and blue-collar communities. On Election Day, Sheila and I were on the speaking platform on the back of the green bus with a bullhorn, urging everyone to vote. We came to the north side of Minneapolis, an inner-city community. I'll never forget the reaction: People were smiling and waving back, in part because so few statewide candidates ever came to their community to ask for their vote, let alone in an old green schoolbus!

There is a simple but important point. The 50 percent hole in the electorate in a presidential election or the 70 percent hole in local elections is stratified by class. Disproportionate among the ranks of nonvoters are "minorities" and blue-collar and low-income citizens. It is the Democrats' natural constituency, *if* we are willing to speak to the concerns and circumstances of their lives and include them. If you don't say anything important to them and hardly ever show up in the community, people don't vote. Why should they?

Somehow, too many Democrats have failed to make a key distinction. It is true, as the conventional wisdom goes, that if you speak only about the poor, you lose. This is fairly obvious. But to say you should not focus only on the poor doesn't mean you should never deal with issues of poverty. The same holds for issues of race and gender. The Democratic Party, which is supposed to be the party of the people, has too often been silent about these issues. To do the right thing *and to win,* they must be put back on the table.

We won the 1996 race because of people like Jeff Blodgett. At age thirty-five, he supervised a staff of about thirty, almost all of them under thirty! The teacher in me, and more important the organizer in me, loved seeing these idealistic young people trounce the Republicans' cynical poison politics. A top-notch field operation is worth between three and nine points in a statewide race. That can be the difference between victory and defeat.

The pundits and political operatives too often minimize the importance of a strong field operation, focusing instead on the importance of message and media strategy. One of our great successes in the 1996 race was our ability to use our field operation as an extension of our message and media strategy. We were able to turn the fact that the Republicans had made me their number one target to our advantage. Up above our campaign headquarters, we put a billboard showing a huge red target and the words "Millions of Republican Dollars Aimed Here." Our volunteers wore T-shirts with targets on the back, reading, "I'm a Republican Target." Another T-shirt that literally sold out in one day at our Minnesota State Fair booth had on the front a political cartoon from the Minneapolis *Star Tribune* drawn by Steve Sack. The cartoon depicted the famous photo of the defiant Chinese dissident standing in front of the Chinese army tanks in Tiananmen Square. Only in this cartoon, I was the one standing in front of a line of tanks that read "Republicans" on the side!

Our volunteers felt ownership of the campaign. They knew the issues and what was at stake in the election. They knew that when the Republicans targeted me, all of my supporters, all of our volunteers, all of our precinct captains, and all of our door knockers had become targets as well.

Finally, the television ads were, as much as I don't like to admit it, also very important. I had to make two very difficult decisions early on in the campaign. The first was that I would have to raise a lot of money. I came very close to deciding that I wouldn't raise any money except what was necessary for the green bus and grassroots campaigning. When all the attack ads started, I would tell Minnesotans, "If you believe all this crap, you should vote against me. But I refuse to spend my time raising money for TV ads—and I have faith in your intelligence and good judgment." We had some long—and loud—debates about this subject. To this day, I still think I might have been able to pull it off—and what a victory that would have been!

Sheila persuaded me that I could not take this kind of chance. She argued, with considerable passion, that too much was at stake—this Senate race was about not one person but rather the future of progressive politics in our state. So I raised money—more than six million dollars. Fortunately, we raised (and spent) most of it through direct mail. This was good because I could not and would not spend hours on the phone begging for money. It is so awful, so demeaning. More than 80 percent of this money was raised in contributions of less than two hundred dollars each. That made me feel better, but it never felt right.

The Republican attack was relentless, and I needed professional help. The second big decision I made was to bring Jim Andrews and Mandy Grunwald to the campaign. Jim managed the overall campaign with Jeff Blodgett. A veteran of many campaigns, this outspoken "political operative" blended in with our grassroots organizing (which he didn't much believe in) and provided the expertise, week by week, on how to respond to the attacks and how to go on the offensive. I was more than ready to take on the Boschwitz and D'Amato campaign on the issues.

Mandy Grunwald, best known for her work in the 1992 Clinton campaign, was a delight to work with. Mandy represented a break from our earlier ad style. She maintained a perfect balance between illustrating the passion I have for the issues and reminding Minnesotans that I had accomplished a lot for our state.

And Mandy respected our wishes. Sheila and I wanted to do an ad dealing with domestic violence but do it in a "talking head" style, which is not supposed to work well. Mandy agreed to give it her best. I sat in a chair, faced the camera, and spoke to people. I told Minnesotans that "every thirteen seconds a woman is battered in her home. A home should be a safe place, and one of the reasons that this happens is that not enough men speak up. As a United States senator from Minnesota, I'll always speak up." This ad was very personal and powerful and, as it turns out, had a huge impact.

The Boschwitz and NRSC ads were slash-and-burn in style and always very personal. Our ads were comparison ads on issues or talking-head ads in which I spoke about issues. The contrast helped us win the election. I can't tell you how many people came up to me after the election and said, "Senator, I don't agree with you on most issues, but I voted for you because of the way you conducted your campaign. You were honest about your positions on issues and you didn't engage in personal attacks." For many voters, their choice is not about ideology—whether one is left, right, or center. It has to do with whether they think you stand up for what you believe in and that, in the end, you are standing up for them.

One other comment I kept hearing during the Republican attacks: "We don't understand. They are spending millions of dollars attacking you for being 'embarrassingly liberal.' But we already know that you are a liberal. That's no big surprise to Minnesotans!"

Diane Feldman was another key outside professional who helped us win. She was my pollster. We laugh about this because she knows how much I hate polling. I did not poll during my first four years in office and agreed to only during the election cycle so we would know how the war was going. I even boycott Senate Democrat meetings when pollsters report on what's popular and what's not. It is like having a weekly spine check to see what we stand for. It is insulting—one of the horrible legacies of the Clinton administration, I think.

But Diane Feldman is special. In 1990, she was one of five people in Washington who was interested in our race. I'll never forget the time she picked me up at the airport in her old, beat-up car, not to mention the mess inside. I said to her, "This is my kind of car. You're hired!" Of course, we had no money then, but she still helped—out of commitment to me and what our campaign stood for. She is a dear friend who was never one point off during the final critical months of the 1996 race. She also gave me the best advice of the campaign: She told me that Minnesotans did not agree with me on every issue, but many of them admired my courage and integrity. I hope and pray that Minnesotans will always feel this way about me.

The final crucial element for success was, believe it or not, the issues. I told Minnesotans I was for universal health care coverage—Medicare for all, living-wage jobs, the right of workers to organize and bargain collectively, more investment in children and education, more environmental protection, and campaign finance reform. In every speech, every debate, every ad, I tried to never equivocate on the issues. I was a liberal and proud of it! But there was also the populism that people seemed to love. We made being the number one target of the Republican Party an advantage—indeed, it was a major theme of our campaign. In every stump speech and whenever I was in front of a camera, I said, "The big insurance companies, pharmaceutical companies, oil companies, grain companies, and tobacco companies don't like me. But they already have great representation in Washington. It is the rest of the people who need it. I represent children, education, farmers, and working families, and I'm proud of it." I know this sounds immodest, but people loved it. And I sure loved saying it.

In the Senate, we come to "the well" to call out our votes, "yea" or "nay." I could write another book about the conversations that take place in the well. One frequent topic is television attack ads. Senators are acutely aware that communications technology has become the main weapon in electoral conflict. A typical refrain is "Can you imagine what the attack ad would look like on this vote?" Quite often, this is another way of saying, "I hate voting this way, but I have no choice if I don't want to lose my next election."

I learned an important lesson from this process. In 1993–1994, I observed one senator closely as he cast several votes he obviously didn't believe in. One time, he came up to me, noticing the disapproval on my face, and said, "Paul, understand, I have to get through this election." This senator had served many distinguished years. I especially admired his ability to manage a bill on the floor. He was thoughtful, articulate, and a great debater. He was a great senator. And yet he was a shell of himself and miserably unhappy that election year. And he lost.

I remember thinking to myself: The worst thing would be to lose your dignity, to vote against your convictions, and lose the next election anyway.

Eventually, I was able to kid other senators that I had cast so many unpopular votes that the Republicans wouldn't have enough money, even with their millions of dollars, to run all the attack ads I'd given them. The ideal is to always vote your conviction. I try to live up to this.

One exception, though I'm still not sure, might be the Defense of Marriage Act (DOMA). This legislation—which said that if one state (in the case at hand, Hawaii) permitted same-sex marriage, the decision could not be binding on other states—was basically an effort to prohibit same-sex marriage.

I felt that changing the definition of marriage went too far for me. The implications were too far-reaching. My own life and lifestyle made me very cautious and conservative in this regard. I had a perfect human rights record and had received awards for leading the fight for gay and lesbian Americans, but I was not prepared to go this far, I thought.

When I was asked about my position on DOMA on a talk-radio show, I stated my view. It was absolutely the worst forum to do so. And while I had told some friends in the community that I could not yet support same-sex marriage, I should never have publicly announced my position without first talking to many others. It was a matter of friendship and sensitivity to a community that had given me great support. I failed miserably on this count.

The gay and lesbian community was stunned when they heard the news. In fact, that day there happened to be a fund-raiser for me sponsored by leaders in the gay and lesbian community in downtown Minneapolis. Some people were very angry. Many more were deeply hurt. It was painful to see my friends disappointed in me.

What troubles me is that I may not have cast the right vote on

DOMA. I might have rationalized my vote by making myself believe that my honest position was opposition. This vote was an obvious trap for a senator like me, who was up for reelection. Did I convince myself that I could gleefully deny Republicans this opportunity? After all, the Supreme Court of Hawaii had not made a decision in its pending case, and there certainly was no danger that other states or the federal government were about to pass legislation supporting same-sex marriage. This was all political.

When Sheila and I attended a Minnesota memorial service for Mathew Shepard, I thought to myself, "Have I taken a position that contributed to a climate of hatred?" Of course, I never believed this when I voted for DOMA. But if you deny people who are in a stable, loving relationship the right to marry, do you deny them their humanity? I still wonder if I did the right thing.

One other issue figured prominently in the 1996 Senate race. On the Friday before the election, Rudy Boschwitz held a press conference to announce that I had burned a flag when I was a student at the University of North Carolina. Since I refused, on First Amendment grounds, to support a constitutional amendment to ban the desecration of the flag, I was vulnerable to this kind of attack. The Republicans had run ads on TV, there were rallies held by the Citizens Flag Alliance, and American Legion leaders were especially angry over this vote. This press conference was meant to be a knockout blow. Actually, it was a desperate tactic by a campaign that was way behind and willing to say or do anything to win.

To the credit of the Minnesota media, they asked the Boschwitz campaign when, where, and how I had burned a flag. The campaign had no answers, no proof, because I never *had* burned a flag! I can only be contemptuous about this attack. When you're a first-generation American, the son of Russian-Jewish immigrants who fled persecution, one thing you would never do is burn a flag. The Minnesota media turned on the Boschwitz campaign. A front-page article in the St. Paul *Pioneer Press* the following day began, "Without offering any concrete evidence, U.S. Senate candidate Rudy Boschwitz called a news conference Friday to suggest that Senator Paul Wellstone participated in the burning of an American flag in the 1960s. No time, date, or place was ever suggested by Boschwitz." But most important, the veterans' community rose up in my defense! I certainly wouldn't have the support of the veterans' community without consistently trying to do well for all people. Our Minnesota office returned every phone call and every letter from veterans. Over and over again, working with county veteran-service officers, we had been able to help veterans and their families. The more we helped, the more calls for help we received. Josh Syrjamaki and Mike Siebenaler of my staff became mythical figures in the veterans' community, known as effective advocates who came through for families. I had had no idea how many veterans needed help, especially good health care. The veterans became my teachers, and their cause became my cause.

All that weekend, veterans traveled throughout Minnesota demanding an apology. The Vietnam Veterans of America, the Paralyzed Veterans of America, the Disabled American Veterans, the National Association of Atomic Veterans, and the Military Order of the Purple Heart had all given me national awards for service to veterans, and Minnesotans saw and heard these veterans, joined by many VFW and American Legion members (who didn't agree with their leaders), demanding an apology. It was very powerful. It was the end of the Boschwitz campaign. We won by nine points.

The Republicans were sure that an outspoken progressive like me would be easy to beat. But we won by asking Minnesotans to vote for what they believed in. I don't expect that Minnesotans will agree with me all the time, but I am proud of the bond I have built with them, and they know that I am on their side. I don't put much faith in polls, but one exit poll done by the Minneapolis *Star Tribune* that Election Day contained some interesting information. A large minority of voters polled said that they felt I was "too liberal." Of those voters, 40 percent voted for me. Among voters who considered themselves "moderates," 59 percent voted for me. The politics of conviction is a winning politics. That's why an "embarrassingly liberal" senator was able to win decisively.

Chapter 7

—

DEMOCRACY
FOR THE FEW

Plutarch wrote of the fall of Rome: "The abuse of buying and selling votes crept in and money began to play an important part in determining elections. Later on, however, this process of corruption spread to the law courts and to the army, and finally, when even the sword became enslaved by the power of gold, the republic was subjected to the rule of emperors."

The way in which money has come to dominate politics is the foremost ethical issue of politics of our time. The corruption is far more serious than any wrongdoing by an individual officeholder. It is systemic corruption, in which there is a huge imbalance of power between the vast majority of the people and those few who have the financial wherewithal to count more. We have as a nation moved dangerously far away from the central principle of representative democracy: Each person counts as one and no more than one.

The philosopher José Ortega y Gasset concluded, "The health of any democracy . . . depends on a small detail: the conduct of elections. Everything else is secondary." In a system in which it costs, on average, more than two thirds of a million dollars to get elected to the House of Representatives and nearly five million dollars to get elected to the Senate, politicians pay close attention to those who have the most money. There is no other choice if you want to get elected. After all, the candidate who spends the most wins nine times out of ten.

I am not saying that as a candidate you feel obligated to take a position on an issue in order to raise money from the big givers (though there is pressure to do so). I am saying that all of us are dependent on money to get elected or reelected, and we are well aware of who can afford to send a large contribution. When we sit down to solicit funds, we work from call lists that say things like: "John Smith and his wife, Betty, can each afford to give $1,000. They are very wealthy and quite liberal. They have a special interest in the environment and human rights." I am certain that *every* senator and representative is given this kind of call list.

If big money talks, early money screams. A candidate has to raise a critical amount of money early in the campaign in order to hire staff, start a field operation, and have at least some presence on television and radio. Many candidates and campaigns never get off the ground because they cannot raise this crucial early money. Large contributions provide the necessary capital faster. Later on, a campaign can do direct-mail solicitation, and if you are known (most of the time this works only for incumbents) you can raise a lot of money in much smaller contributions. But it takes the initial large contributions to raise the small contributions. It takes a lot of money to raise money.

I call those citizens who are the early investors the gatekeepers. They have the power to decide whether or not you as a candidate will be able to run for office. I'll never forget one classic call I made in 1990 to a well-known supporter of progressive politics and a good friend and strong backer of mine now. At the time, he told me, "I know exactly who you are, and you don't have a prayer of winning. I am not interested."

I was frustrated and angry in my quest to become a senator and wanted someone to listen. I asked Doug Grow, a columnist for the Minneapolis *Star Tribune,* to hear me out. He drove to Northfield, and we had coffee at a local café. I railed about the gatekeepers. Their only interest, I told Doug, was whether I could raise millions of dollars to get elected. There was no discussion about content of character, issues, leadership, or vision. Since when did the ability to raise millions of dollars become a qualification to serve in the U.S. Senate?

I told the gatekeepers that I wasn't wealthy and didn't have access to millions of dollars, but that I would launch a grassroots campaign. I wouldn't spend all my time raising money, but I would raise the big issues. I would go directly to people, in the best sense of what democracy is all about. The gatekeepers would look at me, their eyes glazing over. They had no interest, I almost shouted at Doug Grow. I went on to vent my anger at the media. "You all perpetuate this cycle. You repeatedly judge candidate viability by fund-raising reports. The pundits buy into this, and the conventional wisdom is—and what a sad commentary this is—that success comes from money."

I expressed my full indignation. It must have been a strange sight to others who were having coffee there. But I wanted to shout all of this from the mountaintop, and Doug Grow was a patient listener. He wrote a column with the headline THE GATEKEEPERS, probably more to give me some solace and comfort than any other reason. I appreciated his humanity!

Ten years later, it has only gotten worse, especially for the challengers. Worst of all is the current state of the primaries. Indeed, the primary is oversold as a democratic institution. The original idea was that, rather than party bosses at a convention, the people would decide on candidates in a primary. All across the country, we have "wealth primaries" that narrow the choice down to two for the people. I certainly agree with Jon Corzine of New Jersey on many issues. He visited with Democratic senators and said, "My opponent will attack me as being to the left of Paul Wellstone and Ted Kennedy, but I am a real Democrat. I don't intend to retreat from what I believe in." I loved it, but look at how he won the primary: He spent more than thirty million dollars.

Herb Kohl is another telling example. He is my colleague from neighboring Wisconsin and is unpretentious, decent, and very wealthy. Herb ran in the 1988 Democratic primary in Wisconsin against two formidable figures, Governor Tony Earl, a great environmentalist, and Ed Garvey, an articulate populist. Herb dominated the airwaves with unlimited ads bought with his unlimited resources. The tag line of each ad was, "Nobody's senator but your own." So now we come full circle. Herb becomes the reformer because he doesn't have to depend on outside money from wealthy contributors. Since he can finance the election himself, he is not dependent on anyone else. Hence, the people in Wisconsin can be sure that he will belong only to them. Herb blew out his opponents with saturation advertising and went on to win the general election.

The moral to this story (and to too many others) is that there is one way that candidates can stay clear of the obscene money chase, one way that they can spend all of their time with real constituents instead of cash constituencies: Be independently wealthy! But this isn't the answer for a representative democracy. The Senate already is more than 50 percent millionaires. If the trend continues, almost everyone will be disenfranchised from running for office. You are either wealthy or the choice of wealthy contributors.

My reelection campaign in 1996 was a different kind of fundraising nightmare. I didn't have to worry about the gatekeepers any longer. I could more easily raise the necessary money (except from the many financial interests that I had offended!) because I was an incumbent and well known in political circles.

The problem was that as a reformer who hates this system and has tried to change it, I still had to work within it. The Republicans launched harsh attacks, calling me a hypocrite. Ann McBride, then president of Common Cause, came to Minnesota and said in my defense, "We don't ask our heroes to unilaterally disarm. They have no other choice to but raise money in this system. That's why we have to change it." But while the attack never stuck with Minnesotans, it stuck with me. I never felt right raising the money.

Many in the campaign were furious at me for not making more fund-raising calls, but it was torture to me. Every day, I found excuses for not raising money.

I am amazed that more incumbent senators, Democrats and Republicans alike, don't lead the charge for reform. It is true that the system is wired for incumbency, as we easily raise much more money than our opponents, and 95 percent of us get reelected. But the system is so degrading that I would think that incumbents, out of dignity, would pass sweeping campaign-finance-reform legislation.

I haven't talked to one senator of either party who doesn't hate their election cycle. It is a constant money chase. Almost every weekend, senators crisscross the country to attend high-dollar fund-raisers. We see one another on the road. During the week, very distinguished and able people in Congress spend four hours a day, every day, making phone calls for money. They are mainly calling people they don't even know. For my own part, I don't know which is worse—calling perfect strangers or close friends. It is all awful.

And it looks awful. Bill Moyers put it this way in a speech he sent me titled "The Soul of Democracy":

> If a baseball player, stepping up to the plate, were to lean over and hand the umpire a wad of bills before he calls the pitch, we'd know what it was, right? We'd call it a bribe. But when a real estate developer buys his way into the White House with big bucks and gets a favorable government ruling that wouldn't be available to you or me, or when the tobacco industry stuffs $13 mil-

lion in the pockets of Gingrich, Lott and their band of merry loot-
ers, what do we call that? A "campaign contribution."
What we should really call it is a bribe, a legal bribe.

In March 1994, I spoke on the Senate floor about the failing
health of our democracy. I condemned the one hundred million
dollars spent by the medical-industrial complex (the insurance industry, drug companies, HMOs, and medical trade organizations) to
defeat health care reform in our country. I pointed out the dramatic
increase in that industry's PAC and individual contributions to incumbents. I wanted the recipients of this money to feel some dis-
comfort.

I know that at least some of the big givers were uncomfortable.
One early morning in August 1994, during the height of the Senate
health care debate, I spoke to a gathering of 350 orthopedic surgeons. It was not a fund-raiser but a favor to a childhood friend who
was in the field.

I arrived five minutes early, and as I entered the room I heard
the group's PAC director tell the doctors, "When you go to see your
representative or your senator, you cannot give them a PAC check
in their office. That is not legal. So they might want to just tell you
where to send it instead." And then he hesitated and said, in an
awkward way, "But they will take it." There was uneasy laughter in
the room, because these doctors clearly didn't feel good about their
role in the process.

Then I was introduced. I was trying to figure out a transition, as
I thanked these surgeons for their work, mentioning my own ath-
letic injuries and operations. Then I told them that while I would

speak about health care policy, I wanted to respond first to what I had heard. I told them that I didn't think representatives or senators should take any health care PAC money before voting on health care legislation. I was certain these remarks would be met with a wall of hostility. Instead, to my surprise, the surgeons literally came to their feet and gave me a long standing ovation. Their reaction made me hopeful: People feel ripped off, and they are angry—even prosperous orthopedic surgeons!

The current system makes all of us look bad. Every time John McCain comes to the floor and points the finger at big money as the explanation for senators' votes on legislation, I think to myself, "John, people could say the same about you or any of us." McCain receives a tremendous amount of money from powerful financial interests that come under his jurisdiction as chair of the Commerce Committee.

The same applies to Russ Feingold or me. It can be argued that we take strong labor or environmental stands because we receive money from these organizations. And even if I honestly and truthfully believe that this has never happened nor will ever happen, it doesn't always look that way to the people we represent. I understand why they are often skeptical.

Most people in public office argue that the causality goes the other way. They don't vote a particular way for campaign contributions, rather, the contributions flow in because of the way they vote and the positions they take. I don't see this as much of an improvement.

The money chase creates another problem that is rarely discussed. I think it is one of the worst aspects of fund-raising. How can we be the best senators for our constituents when for two years prior to each election we spend four or five hours a day dialing for dollars? We miss committee hearings, meet with fewer constituents, are less prepared on the issues, and are less often on the floor debating and advocating and fighting for the people who elected us. This is wrong. Of course, the incumbents, unless they are wealthy, have no choice but to raise money if they want to get reelected.

Another huge problem for representative democracy is the source of the money. Only a spectacularly small portion of the U.S. population contributes more than two hundred dollars to a political campaign, much less one thousand dollars. In the first half of 1999, fewer than four out of every ten thousand Americans (0.037 percent) made a contribution greater than two hundred dollars, and only 0.022 percent of all Americans had given one thousand dollars to a presidential candidate. And yet this small group spent close to two thirds of a billion dollars in the 1998 election. Another quarter billion came in large gifts from corporations, wealthy individuals, and unions in the form of "soft money."

These moneyed voices get heard in Washington. When big contributors call members of Congress, their calls are returned. When Senator Paul Simon had a list of calls to return at the end of the day, he started with those who he knew were generous donors. He wasn't proud of it, but it was true. If Simon, a committed reformer who epitomized integrity in public life, succumbed to this fund-raising logic, just imagine the conduct of others.

Sometimes I get pressured into attending a DSCC fund-raiser: "Paul, you need to support your colleagues who are up for reelection. We need you there to stand by them." At these events, it is just amazing how people mix money, politics, and policy without any hesitation. They come up to you, give you their business card, and launch into a discussion about their concerns, even about upcoming Senate votes!

At one of these receptions, a big giver, who was originally from India, approached me. "Senator," he said, "I know you are opposed to exporting any more military weapons to Pakistan [in general, I am opposed to exporting more arms anyplace], and if you would go to the floor and speak about this, I can raise you a lot of money." He was just trying to help, not to do anything dishonest, but I was horrified. I felt as if I had broken some law by just listening to him. To me, it felt like an offer of a bribe. I was so paranoid about this conversation that I never spoke one word on the subject in the debate, even though I had intended all along to take part in it.

The moneyed interests slip easily into the back rooms where policy is made, and they shape the congressional agenda. If you had walked into the anteroom of the Senate chamber during consideration of the massive telecommunications bill of 1996, you would have seen lobbyists for the many varied business interests packed wall to wall, but you would have searched in vain for representatives of consumers, of ordinary people. This was critically important legislation that would affect cable rates and, most important, concentrations of power in the industry—the control of information in a democracy. The proposed legislation would permit further concentration of media ownership, on the grounds that information technologies would ensure widespread dispersal of news. But this argument begged the question of control. If you believe that citizens should have access to a broad range of political perspectives, concentrated media lead to a poorly functioning democracy.

The American people were not invited to be part of this debate, and the media conglomerates provided scant information to the public. People didn't have a clue about the legislation, which passed. It was a slam dunk for the powerful telecommunications lobby and a knockout punch to representative democracy.

Big money undercuts representative democracy at every turn. Powerful economic interests have the capital to hire lobbyists that march on Washington every day. Powerful lobbying coalitions in Washington exert tremendous power—they have easy access to legislators and their staffs, as well as to the executive branch. They use their money, expertise, media contacts, status, and prestige to frame and define the issues. These lobbying coalitions define for senators and representatives what is practical, reasonable, and commonsensical. Just look at the bankruptcy bills passed by the House and the Senate. I was told that committee staff refer to the bills' various provisions based on which industry "paid" for them. This provision is for the credit-card companies, this one for the real-estate industry, and so on. As *The Wall Street Journal* noted in April 2000,

> Lawmakers like to portray the battle over bankruptcy reform as a clash of principles: stopping debtors from shirking their obligations or creditors from fleecing the needy. But in the back rooms of Capitol Hill, the nature of the fight changes. Industry lobbyists, many ostensibly allied in favor of bankruptcy overhaul legislation, vie to carve out as many favors for their clients as possible at the expense of other business groups. These contests pit auto companies against credit card issuers, retailers against realtors and the Delaware bar against lawyers from the rest of the United States.

Again, the major winners in all of this seem to be the major political parties—certainly not low- and moderate-income debtors. Contributions from the lending industry to both parties since 1997 top twenty million dollars.

Interests of ordinary people often go unheard. Few lobby on behalf of the poor and needy. During debate on the 1996 welfare-reform bill, Senator Daniel Patrick Moynihan, the Democratic floor manager and defender of the poor, bemoaned the comparative silence on the bill:

> The lobbies are empty. There is no outcry against what we are doing. Two fine editorials appeared this morning in *The Washington Post* and *The New York Times* saying, "Do not do this." But those are rare voices at this moment....
>
> Actually, there is one unified voice: that of every national religious and faith-based charity.... Other organizations, as I say, are once again silent. Having briefly aroused themselves, they have sunk back into apathy, or resignation—or agreement with what is about to be done. We will not know if we do not hear.

Pat Moynihan had every right to ask, "Where is the indignation in the country against this harsh legislation?" But the larger point is that advocates for the poor have few of the resources—money, access, status, prestige—that add up to political clout in Washington. The truth of the matter is, most ordinary citizens are shut out. If the political system actually worked for the majority, then certainly much more would already have been done for education, affordable child care, and health security for families. Congress would pass sweeping campaign finance reform as well.

We do not have true democracy because our political system does not work for the people. Instead, well-paid corps of lobbyists and moneyed interests perpetuate the status quo. These power brokers rob the people of their ability to exercise authority, at least in free and open elections in which the best ideas and the best candidates prevail.

Government too often fails to hear the voices of the people, while it listens too closely to special interests:

• Government tolerates and sometimes worsens inequality, while it heeds wealthy campaign contributors.

• Americans do not have universal health coverage, while HMOs, insurance companies, and other health-industry lobbyists spent hundreds of millions on Washington politicians in 1997 alone.

• Many in Congress advocate plans to privatize some or all of Social Security, plans that would see as much as a fifth of the returns on investment go to the brokerage industry in the form of fees, while investment interests led the list of donors to Republican national committees in the 1998 election cycle.

• Improvements in the minimum wage and workplace standards face an uphill battle in Congress, while businesses give politicians eleven times more political contributions than unions do.

As the influence of power brokers has risen, so has the disenchantment of voters. When the people don't hear politicians talk about their concerns, they drop out. The 1998 election motivated barely 36 percent of the electorate to vote, the lowest turnout since 1942, and the lowest turnout outside of the South since 1818. Despite an increase in registered voters, twenty-two million fewer Americans voted in 1998 than in 1994, continuing a long-term decline that has spanned nearly four decades. As *The Wall Street Journal*'s Gerald Seib wrote, "It's often said that Congress is the voice of the people. More accurately, it has become the voice of one in five people."

The money chase, combined with this record-low voter turnout, has a lethal effect on politics. Most politicians dare not take positions that will offend the dominant economic interests and have little to say to or for low- and moderate-income people. These citizens thus become even further alienated from politics, there is even lower turnout, and politicians pay even less attention. It is a vicious cycle that is destroying representative democracy.

There has been much discussion of President Clinton's fundraising. But there has been little analysis of the Clinton-Gore administration's legacy for the Democratic Party. Unfortunately, I think the president too often tailored his policies and programs to commercial imperatives, failing to engage ordinary citizens. Clinton helped shape a Democratic Party that some believe has little purpose other than winning elections. Ordinary citizens know this and are uninspired.

So many young people I meet are profoundly cynical about politics. Many have no interest in it. Those that do think that they will never run for office because of the fund-raising challenges. They are committed to public service but think they have no chance of serving. This is not the way it is supposed to be in a representative democracy. I don't know which is worse—people so turned off that they won't even vote, or men and women who are excited about public affairs but will never run for public office because of money. Many in both major parties now call for campaign finance reform. Congress has focused on proposals, like the McCain-Feingold bill, that limit some of the worst abuses. I was, along with Senator Fred Thompson of Tennessee, an original cosponsor of this legislation, but the experience has been discouraging. The original bill is so whittled down that it doesn't even apply spending limits to congressional races. The focus is on abolishing "soft money," which would move us forward but would be only a modest first step. So far, we haven't even been able to pass this incremental reform.

My concern is that there will be a deal in which getting rid of soft money is exchanged for *raising* contribution limits. The argument is that these limits have not kept up with inflation and that candidates would have to make fewer calls if they could raise larger amounts of money from each call. But raising contribution limits would only exacerbate the disparity between the average citizen and the moneyed citizen.

Only a tiny percentage of voting citizens can afford to make large hard-money contributions, to say nothing of soft-money contributions. If money equals speech, it is easy to see who is doing all the talking and who are the folks senators and representatives are listening to. The hopes, dreams, concerns of the vast majority of people are going unheard because the thousand-dollar bullhorn drowns them out. Why would we want to make that bullhorn bigger and louder? Why would we want to give greater access and more control to those who already have it locked up?

On present course, I can see such a deal happening. It would be legislation with a made-for-Congress look—a great acronym with very little effect. The claim will be, "We've done campaign reform now for the new millennium." Meanwhile, the mixing of big money and politics will go on at record pace.

People outside Washington, D.C., are ready for a bolder response. They feel ripped off by a system that requires you to pay to play. The people want real elections instead of what are in effect auctions.

"Clean money" campaign reform—already enacted in Massachusetts, Arizona, Maine, and Vermont—offers real hope for driving big-money power brokers out of election campaigns and inviting ordinary citizens back into effective participation in politics. In keeping with Supreme Court rulings, clean-money campaign reform presents a strictly voluntary system but one with strong incentives for candidates to participate. Candidates who choose to reject private money and limit their spending receive a set amount of "clean money" from a publicly financed fund. This plan allows qualified candidates to run for public office without compromising their independence.

A delegation of Maine politicians, Democrats and Republicans, incumbents and challengers, came to my office to share their experience under this new system. They were proud of it. The incumbents knew they had given up an advantage, but they felt free—free to raise the big issues and not the big money. All of them said it was the right thing to do. And they reported that people were constantly thanking them for being clean candidates. I hope they all win, including the Republicans, because they will all be much better representatives, free from much of the influence of private money. This has to be the future for American politics.

People have become so used to the system that they don't even realize what they're doing any longer. It's just assumed that you do what you have to do, and you don't even stop to think how awful it all is.

Even among people who hate the money chase, even among reformers—these are not always the same thing, but there's a fair amount of overlap—the expectations for the success of reform are so low. So some people simply surrender. That's why the energy for this, the motive power for reform, must be external. For even reformers wonder in their heart of hearts whether reform can win in Washington.

I try to support these organizing efforts every way I can. It is a great feeling to visit different states and validate, legitimate, and hopefully inspire this work.

Within the limited measures being considered in Washington, a ban on soft money would be significant reform, but I do not believe it is the best we can do. My priority is to pass an amendment to McCain-Feingold that will allow states to enact voluntary systems of public financing for federal candidates. This way, states could apply "clean money, clean election" laws not only to state races but also to U.S. House and Senate races. I will force a vote on this question, making sure that every senator is on record for or against allowing his or her state to decide to do this. It would be tough for a senator to vote against this proposition. States should be allowed to consider moving forward where fainter hearts in Washington fear to proceed. I am convinced that while we don't yet have the political muscle to pass sweeping campaign finance reform in Washington, we can win at the state level. That is how we can turn this whole rotten system upside down—or, rather, right side up.

We can't wait for those inside the system to bring about the change. The American people are regularly treated to the spectacle of the party conventions awash in special-interest money. In 2000, the telecommunications companies, for example, were big underwriters for dozens of costly receptions for top lawmakers. AT&T gave one million dollars' worth of goods and services to each party convention. These firms have huge stakes in government decisions concerning mergers, access to airwaves, and other regulations.

It was obscene, but party and political leaders seemed not to notice. They have become so used to this system that they don't see any conflict of interest. It looks awful and reinforces every negative view people have about political parties and politicians; the political class doesn't give this a second thought. It is all part of the way they conduct the business of politics.

To press the case for reform, I spoke at both Shadow Conventions, alternative gatherings in Philadelphia and Los Angeles that featured fired-up coalitions of reformers, environmental and economic-justice activists, and political independents and third-party advocates. I am all for turning up the heat.

While I was in Los Angeles, I met with a group of workers from Loews Hotels. It was quite a contrast from all the money and glitz at the Democratic convention. We met at one of the workers' homes. This small place had three bedrooms; a family lived in each one. Though these families had little money, they cooked a huge Mexican breakfast for me. That was *their* gift.

We talked for over an hour. I mainly listened. The workers said they needed higher wages to support their families. There were especially upset about the working conditions and said being treated fairly was even more important than wages. They all spoke about making a better life for their children. I was very moved by these Latino/Latina workers. They were poetic when talking about their children, and they spoke with such feeling.

The owner of Loews, Jonathan Tisch, is a huge contributor to the Democrats and a friend of Al Gore's. Too many in the Democratic Party do not seem to care that he is in a pitched battle with these workers to keep them from organizing with the Hotel Employees and Restaurant Employees Union (HERE). Will Democrats stand— in actions, not words—for the right of workers to organize and bargain collectively? Will my party commit itself to long-needed labor reform? Or will the money chase gut the "Party of the People"?

This one story tells a much larger story about the Democratic Party and politics in our country. Ordinary citizens know they are shut out. The road leads to plutocracy. Not "government of the people, by the people, and for the people" but government of the few, by the few, and for the few.

It is not that people don't want to change this system. They do. The problem is that the majority of people are convinced it will never change, that big money will always run politics. This sense of powerlessness corrupts. What could be accomplished is never attempted.

The challenge is to mobilize millions of Americans from all walks of life to participate actively in a historic movement to restore our democracy. We need to invite ordinary citizens back into American politics to work for what is right for our nation.

Chapter 8

—

U.S. SENATORS
AND THEIR WORLD

The Veterans Administration appropriations bill was on the floor. I had introduced legislation to assist atomic veterans, those soldiers who in the early 1950s had participated in atomic-bomb tests in Utah and Nevada. They had been required to observe and measure the effects of the bombs, which exposed them to large amounts of radiation. My amendment would put the Senate on record as saying that atomic veterans should receive medical care and compensation for radiogenic diseases. It was only a "sense of the Senate" amendment, which was not binding, but it was important to show support and pave the way for real change.

Kit Bond, senator from Missouri and chair of the housing committee, said the Republicans would accept this amendment on a voice vote. But if I insisted on a recorded vote, he informed me, he would move to table the amendment. The whole point of this exercise was to hold everyone accountable, so I said no. I wanted everyone on record.

Bond opposed the amendment. The majority leader, Trent Lott, cast an early vote against it. Democrats were for it, but Democrats were not the majority. Yet by the time the voting was over, seventy-five senators had sided with me. How did this happen?

Take Missouri's John Ashcroft as an example. Ashcroft, who is very conservative, did not know much about the atomic veterans, and he and I were certainly not political allies! I spoke to him as he approached the clerk to vote. "John," I said, "I promise you the government has mistreated these veterans. They were exposed to massive dosages of radiation, never told they were in danger, and many of them have died of or are very ill from cancer. It is an injustice. They deserve treatment and compensation. I've been working on this for five years, and I don't want to lose this vote. It would be a real setback. Please support me." He chose to trust me. He was the first Republican to vote with me. John's vote was based on a personal relationship. I made a personal appeal, and on this issue he trusted me. That is the only way to explain the vote. I made the same appeal to Tim Hutchinson, Jeff Sessions, Orrin Hatch, Bob Bennett, and other conservatives. They, too, voted with me.

It is amazing how much of what happens in the Senate is based on what Donald R. Matthews, in his pioneering book *U.S. Senators and Their World,* written in 1959, calls "norms and folkways," the unwritten rules that govern behavior. The Senate is a small body, and personal relationships are extremely important in it. It is fine to rock the boat, as I often do, but if people think you are a fraud or just a showboat, they will look for the opportunity to vote no every time your name is on an amendment, and then you are in big trouble. In the ideal situation, others believe in you even when they don't believe in your positions.

When I first came to Washington, in January 1991, I was determined to make an impact, but I made some terrible rookie mistakes. It was an unusual time because Congress was dealing with a life-and-death foreign-policy question: Should we go to war with Iraq? I had not opposed military preparation, but I was adamantly opposed to a congressional resolution approving military action. We had not, I believed, exhausted all diplomatic remedies. War, to me, was the last option. My maiden speech on the Senate floor was on this topic. As I spoke, I wasn't nervous but more in awe of how serious this debate was. And I was one of only one hundred people in our country who could debate and decide! During this time, the U.S. Senate was at its best. Every senator spoke. Most of the speeches were eloquent. There was honest and heartfelt disagreement. The debate was civil and important.

I was not wrong in opposing military action. It became very difficult, however, to oppose the war after it began. I was not able to make it clear that I opposed the mission but not the men and women performing the mission. When your loved one is in harm's way and your senator is speaking out against his or her mission, it seems as if he is not supporting you. This hurt me with many Minnesotans.

My biggest mistake prior to the beginning of military action was going to the Vietnam Veterans Memorial to speak out against the war. I was the only challenger to beat an incumbent in 1990, had just come to Washington in my old green bus, and therefore my first moves were attracting tremendous media attention. We held our press conference not at the wall but about thirty yards away. The National Park Service told us that this was where press conferences were held. I never should have held a press conference anywhere near this sacred memorial. I wanted to dramatize the dangers of military action. Instead, I deeply hurt many Vietnam veterans—really, all of the veterans' community. The media coverage was highly critical—how could it be otherwise?—and in a few short weeks I went from rising star to falling star. Minnesotans were ashamed of me. One columnist reported that I had become "a pariah." My approval rating in the polls fell to 38 percent. There were threats on my life. I wished I had never been elected. I felt that I had embarrassed my family and my friends. How could I have been so insensitive to Vietnam vets and to their families?

The media coverage was brutal, even after things began to change for the better. Six months later, the *Today* show wanted to see how I was doing in Minnesota. A reporter followed me around over a long weekend and then called me a few days later to report on her informal poll. The vast majority of Minnesotans she had talked with were favorable. I told her somewhat kiddingly, "Let me know when this is on. It has been a long time since there has been a positive story, and I want to call my kids so they can see it."

She called back a few days before the story was to run with an apology. NBC didn't want her story, she said. Instead, they ran a highly negative one, with no mention of Minnesotans' forgiveness of my blunder. The story closed with Bryant Gumbel asking Lisa Myers: "Does anyone in the Senate take him seriously?" She replied, "Not really."

I later heard that Pat Moynihan, whom I didn't know well then, called NBC to challenge their report. "How do you know he is not taken seriously by other senators? Have you asked any of us?" he asked. He felt it was unfair and unkind to say this without any evidence. I called Senator Moynihan to thank him for his kindness.

Then there was Howard Metzenbaum, the tough, outspoken liberal senator from Ohio. Metzenbaum, in his mid-seventies, with a lot of experience under his belt, approached me on the floor of the Senate. "I've been reading your press," he said. "It's terrible. I want you to come by my office."

I dropped by his office the next day. He shut the door and asked me to sit down. He said to me, "I've been through some tough fights and difficult times in my life. Do you know what I do during these difficult times? I pick out the busiest block in Cleveland. As I walk down the sidewalk, all sorts of people are passing me by. I look at each one of them and say to myself, 'Screw you!' " I believe this was Senator Metzenbaum's way of telling me to have confidence in myself. It's certainly difficult to forget such advice.

Paul Simon from Illinois had a different style. Week after week during these horrible first six months, he assured me that things would get better and that I was destined to be a great senator. Paul Simon was my best friend in the Senate. When Paul retired in 1996, it left a real hole for me. I still call him for advice.

At first, I gravitated to Paul because he was so generous with advice and support. Sometimes, I had the most difficult time with liberal senators, who made it clear that child care or education or labor were *their* issues. It became a turf fight, which was disillusioning. Paul was the opposite—always encouraging and supportive. When I wanted to introduce right-to-organize legislation, Paul, who had worked in this area, immediately suggested we work together—he had no use for claims of rank, seniority, or ownership.

Early on, Paul also taught me that unpopular votes did not mean the end of your career. When others cast the easy vote, saying it wasn't worth losing an election over an issue—and then said the same thing over and over again on many tough issues—Paul told me that people in Illinois supported him for voting his conscience. When I seemed to be all alone on a vote, Paul would give me much reassurance. Later on, we became peers. On the really tough votes, we sought each other's advice. I was always sure that his decision was based on principle, not political expediency.

Most important, Paul taught me the importance of enjoying your work and enjoying your colleagues. These are hard things for me to do. I don't find some senators lovable, and I am always ready to take people on and fight for what I believe in. My philosophy is to push hard every day in the Senate, even if some people are offended. Indeed, I think sometimes Paul didn't appreciate enough the importance of conflict. But he reminded me of the critical distinction between disagreement and destruction. Paul genuinely liked and respected other senators, even those with whom he disagreed profoundly. They knew that, and that is why he was held in such high regard.

Paul Simon helped me become a better senator, but I'm sure most senators, Democrats and Republicans, were not impressed at first with me. That was OK if it was because I was taking them on and challenging power in Washington. It was not OK if it was because I was making stupid and reckless mistakes.

One late night in March, the Senate was about to have a voice vote over allocating twenty billion more dollars for savings-and-loan bailouts. A voice vote meant there would be no recorded vote. Since most senators felt the money was necessary but knew this would be an unpopular vote, they were not anxious to be on the record. This was not a party decision but a "gentleman's agreement" that they all would benefit this way. I thought it was too regular a practice, doing voice votes on really tough issues.

George Mitchell, then the majority leader, asked for "unanimous consent" that this be a voice vote. I objected. To have power in the Senate, you need to know only two words: *I object.* Much of the Senate work—procedural agreements, the passing of bills and amendments, the confirmation of presidential appointments— is done by unanimous consent. If you object, *you have power*— positive or negative depending on the situation.

I demanded a recorded roll call vote on this S&L bailout. I felt very strongly that every senator should be accountable for his or her vote and that it was unconscionable for the Senate as an institution to conduct business this way.

The reaction was swift and decisive. Mitchell, whom I admired, suggested that there was "the absence of a quorum." The ensuing quorum call, during which time the Senate could not conduct business, gave Mitchell and others time to talk with me.

For the next hour (it seemed like eternity), a wave of Democratic senators confronted me. One said, "What makes you so self-righteous?" Another said, "Why don't you just leave the chamber for a minute and we can do this. Who do you think you are?" Another senator said, "You obviously don't know how to get along with people here, and this is going to hurt your work. If you make us vote on this, I'm not going to forget." This was rough!

Another group of senators came over with Robert Byrd, chairman of the appropriations committee. "Senator Byrd," they said, "tell Senator Wellstone what a big mistake he is making." This was not subtle, given Robert Byrd's immense power over, for example, all appropriations requests, including those for Minnesota!

Finally, there was Majority Leader Mitchell. Always brilliant, he argued his brief, making the compelling case that, in calling for a recorded vote, I would defeat my own objectives and make matters worse. I don't remember his words exactly, but after a one-hour pounding I was more than ready to think he was right.

The problem is that the Senate, during these really difficult moments of decision, is your only reality. You can easily forget what Minnesotans in the Town Talk Café in Willmar might tell you. An appeal or an argument from the majority leader is tough to turn down, but the threats, as always, made me more determined.

I still insisted on a roll call vote. One senator, in anger, said to me, "It is easy for you—you're going to vote against it." I cast my vote in a loud and clear voice, "Yea." This was stupid. I was against the bailout, but I wanted to prove to him and others that my greater principle was reform and accountability. I didn't need to prove anything, but emotions were running high.

The next morning, I received a phone call from Senator Connie Mack, a Republican from Florida. He told me he respected me for what I had done. "We were watching you from our side of the aisle. We saw them beating up on you and were wondering if you would break. You didn't, and it took a lot of guts." The norms and folkways of the U.S. Senate!

Philip Brasher wrote an Associated Press story about what happened. Jim Klobuchar, a highly respected columnist for the Minneapolis *Star Tribune,* praised me for standing up to the Senate on behalf of ordinary citizens. In Minnesota, I was a hero! (The occasional disconnect between beliefs in Congress and public sentiment is a serious problem.) Sheila and I went for walks, and Minnesotans would yell out of their cars and pickup trucks, "Ready to give 'em hell, Paul?" Or, "Thanks for standing up for us!" It was amazing and made me feel both good and bad. I felt bad because I didn't want to feed into an across-the-board bashing of the U.S. Senate or public service. I felt good for obvious reasons.

This was a significant reform victory. Indeed, because of this precedent, there is now an understanding that we must have a recorded vote somewhere on all appropriations and controversial legislation. This way, I no longer have to deal with pressure from senators on this issue.

Several weeks after the S&L vote, I had an opportunity to fight for Minnesota. A tornado had cut through the west-central part of the state, causing massive devastation. The town of Chandler, population 350, was practically leveled. It was a miracle that only one person died. The people were desperate for help.

But the Federal Emergency Management Agency (FEMA) was a disaster itself back then (in July 1992) and slow to help. It was an example of government bureaucracy at its worst—slow, insensitive, unresponsive. (Under the subsequent leadership of James Lee Witt, FEMA has become a far more effective and responsive agency.)

When a disaster-relief bill to provide more than one billion dollars in relief to riot-torn Los Angeles came to the Senate floor, I focused attention on the problems in Minnesota. I introduced an amendment to provide immediate relief to these Minnesota communities and threatened to hold up this bill until I'd been assured of aid to our state. I held the floor for several hours, describing the damage in our communities and the need for immediate help. Ted

Stevens, the Republican senator from Alaska and powerful ranking member of the appropriations committee, indicated his displeasure with these tactics: "This is outrageous and irresponsible. The senator from Minnesota is delaying *emergency* assistance for the city of Los Angeles, help they need right now." My response was, "Right now I care more about the small town of Chandler, Minnesota, than Los Angeles."

I told Senator Stevens, in floor debate, that I had no choice but to block this relief bill until I received a solid commitment from FEMA and other federal agencies, such as the Small Business Administration and Farmers Home Administration, that there would be immediate help for Minnesota communities.

After I had held the floor for several hours, these agencies faxed the Senate written assurances of immediate help. I read their statements on the floor, said this was what I was waiting for, and let the Los Angeles relief bill pass. Right after the debate was over, Ted Stevens headed straight for me. "That is exactly what I would have done for Alaska," said Stevens. "That's the way you get things done around here."

The Minneapolis *Star Tribune* carried a story the next day questioning these tactics. The reporter argued that while I had helped some Minnesota communities that desperately needed assistance, I was using up goodwill with other senators and damaging my effectiveness. This kind of confrontation, he argued, would wear thin. But these were the norms and folkways of the Senate—this journalist didn't get it.

Dale Bumpers, the experienced and colorful senator from Arkansas (and the best orator in the Senate), explained this to me the next day. "Paul," Bumpers said, "let me tell you something. You know all those speeches you've given on the Senate floor—they've been good. And every senator is delighted. Because they don't mean anything. Only when you know the rules, know your leverage, and know how to fight are you taken seriously. Now, you are meaner than a junkyard dog. Now you know the rules, and now you are taken seriously."

I could feel good about Bumpers's comment except it meant that for the first year and a half, my oratory on the Senate floor may not have had the impact I thought! Maybe this explains an early encounter with Fritz Hollings, the junior senator (at age sixty-nine!) from South Carolina. I had just given a speech on the floor and felt pretty good—I had spoken with passion and eloquence, I thought. Senator Hollings came up to me and said, "Young man, you remind me of Hubert Humphrey." I was really proud and ready to burst when he went on to say, "You talk too much." Again, I had tripped on an unwritten rule of the Senate.

My legislative director, Mike Epstein, was my teacher. Despite being a political science professor, I had no knowledge of the rules of the Senate, and I had a lot of learning to do. Mike's experience in the Justice Department under Bobby Kennedy and the decades he spent working in the Senate made him a master of Senate rules.

With Mike by my side, I could hold my own with any senator on procedure. I depended on Mike too much in the beginning. It took Senator Alan Simpson, the colorful and astute Republican from Wyoming, to point this out to me. After a good victory on the floor, Alan came up to me, pointed to the Republican side of the aisle, and said, "Paul, you see those senators over there? They've been observing you. They see Mike too close by your side while you're doing things. It doesn't look good. The trick is to have him far enough away that it looks like you're doing everything on your own, but close enough that if they throw a whizzer on you, he will be right there to help." You may laugh, but I've followed his advice!

One place in the legislative process where you are on your own is committee "markup" of bills. Markup is when a committee writes a bill. Most of the work is done by staff members before the committee meets. There are intense debates and negotiations that go on for months, maybe even a year or more. It is true, whether senators want to admit it or not, that staff members have enormous power and directly write most legislation. They receive direction from their bosses, but they have most of the expertise, and we are dependent on them. If you don't have great staffers who have substantive knowledge and are tough, shrewd negotiators, you will have very little impact on legislation.

When a committee meets, it is to deal with all the unresolved issues over which we could not agree. Senators offer amendments, and there can be real debate. You have to be ready to defend your amendment under sharp questioning. It is not like floor debate, which rarely happens. Some senators offer their amendments, then give a supporting speech, wait for other senators to speak for or against their amendments, and then respond with another presentation. But they will not, while speaking, "yield for a question," which means they can avoid direct give-and-take. Other senators do yield to questions and relish the debate; I respect these senators and don't think much of the others.

One evening, after the Republicans blocked voter-registration reform, I came to the Senate floor and started blasting away. I went on for some time about the need to make it easier for citizens to register to vote and expand democracy. The Republicans, I argued, wanted to depress voter turnout, especially among the poor and minorities. I also carried on about how the minority was by filibuster blocking the majority will. Republicans would not agree to a time limit on debate, insisting on their right to unlimited debate. It would take sixty votes to break a filibuster. Democrats were in the majority then. These days, filibusters look pretty good to me!

After I had spent about an hour excoriating the Republicans on C-SPAN, Republican leader Robert Dole must have told Alan Simpson, the Republican whip, to get out and respond. Simpson, known for his wit, intellect, and sharp tongue, did so. And we really went at each other. I know this issue well and was confident, but Alan Simpson was not the kind of senator who shies from debate. It was a very intense discussion but not personal.

We finished about two hours later, and Simpson said, with real excitement, "That was a great debate. Isn't that the way you imagined the Senate would be?" That *is* the way I imagined the Senate would be, but I can remember, over ten years, very few real debates like it.

Markup is different. I remember June 1994, when the Senate Labor and Human Resources Committee (called the Kennedy committee after its chairman, Ted Kennedy) marked up a universal health coverage bill. These were two of the best weeks I've spent in the Senate. Over two weeks, we met about eight hours a day. When a member introduced an amendment, there was sure to be debate. I was impressed with everyone; we were all immersed in health care policy and were well able to argue our points of view. Again, our aides were critically important. While members of the committee were very knowledgeable, it is also true that when the tough questions came, you could see staffers whispering in the ears of *each* of us, providing crucial information and arguments.

The Senate Labor and Human Resources Committee was dealing with public policy that crucially affected people's lives. There were eighteen committee members—ten Democrats and eight Republicans. All were active participants. The issues were exciting. The discussion was stimulating. Every night and early each morning I spent hours getting ready for the markup sessions, preparing to debate different amendments and especially preparing to introduce and defend my own amendments. I was especially pleased that the final bill included language that allowed states to adopt single-payer plans and provisions that assured mental health and substance-abuse treatment. I felt that I had made a real difference, doing something that would dramatically improve people's lives.

The "Kennedy bill" was the first national health insurance legislation to ever come to the floor of the Senate. That should have been enough of a clue to me of what might happen. The United States was (and is) the only advanced economy in the world that did not have some form of national health insurance, and this is testimony to the power of the health industry.

George Mitchell, the Senate majority leader, was committed to passing this legislation. Indeed, he gave up an opportunity to be considered for a Supreme Court seat in order to stay in the Senate and fight for this reform. The Republicans filibustered, but Mitchell kept us in session week after week, even when August recess came.

Republicans were unified in their attack, and they successfully killed the legislation. They were backed by a powerful industry that, through saturation ads and powerful lobbyists, was able to create a climate in which senators could vote against reform and not worry. Whatever money and help they needed would be there. This sounds rather cynical, but it is an accurate analysis.

To be fair, it is also true that some senators, regardless of money and power considerations, were adamantly opposed to any government involvement in health care. Our solution was their nightmare. And they fought hard for what they honestly believed in.

The bitter irony to me is that Democrats, not Republicans, paid the price for the failure of Congress to pass meaningful health care reform. The first year after the 1994 election was horrific. It almost seemed as though Newt Gingrich was president. To his credit, Gingrich was a leader. He had a bold legislative agenda, and he intended to pass it. Democrats were in disarray. Many were ducking for cover. Indeed, it took President Clinton a long time to challenge this extreme agenda, which was an attack on environmental protection, Medicare, and especially the poor, too many of whom were children.

I am proud of my work as a senator during this time, even though I was only stopping the worst, not doing the better. I practically lived on the Senate floor during the first two months of the new Republican majority in the Senate. (Dale Bumpers kidded me that he had instructed his staff to analyze how much time I had been on the floor.) On almost every piece of legislation they introduced, I introduced an amendment that "the United States Senate goes on record that we will take no action that will increase poverty or hunger among children." I also introduced amendments that called for a child-impact statement or analysis of every bill they introduced. Believe it or not, I was defeated even on this symbolic amendment the first couple of times. But it gave me a great opportunity to debate and raise hell. It was the community organizer in me. I wanted to embarrass the Republicans, and I desperately wanted Democrats to fight back.

After several months, this strategy began to work. I even won a vote. One time, Senator Dole, the majority leader, came to the floor in anger at my usual amendment. He pointed out that he had played a crucial role during the 1960s and early 1970s in passing antihunger legislation. He said he cared as much as any senator about this issue and didn't need to be lectured. My response was, "Then vote for my amendment. How can any senator be against it?" I think Senator Dole decided to end what seemed to him to be a never-ending debate. Indeed, a *New York Times Magazine* story quoted him as complaining to the Republican caucus that he was frustrated "with all the press we're giving Wellstone."

I did not change the course of policy. Republicans cut low-income programs. They passed the "welfare reform" bill. But it was important to fight hard and remind Democrats of what we stand for.

The most important battle was over rescissions—proposed budget cuts of existing programs. The Republican majority went further than cutting future budgets—they reached back and cut current operating programs, all in the name of deficit reduction. But this was deficit reduction based on the path of least political resistance: They targeted programs that helped the most politically vulnerable citizens.

In the House, the Republicans had no trouble—the rules enable the majority to roll over the minority. And too many Democrats, still reeling from the election, didn't fight very hard. But in the Senate, if you know the rules and know your leverage, you can make a difference. I was on fire about the proposed cuts in low-income energy assistance, elimination of the TRIO education outreach program, and cuts in senior-citizen counseling assistance for low-income Medicare recipients (which helps seniors understand Medicare rules and regulations). Low-income energy assistance was a lifeline program in a cold-weather state such as Minnesota. Without it, many Minnesotans, including children and the elderly, would be cold or without enough money for food or Medicare. The TRIO program was heart and soul to me. It was an extremely effective outreach program to high schools and middle schools that encouraged "minority" and low-income students to aspire and apply to college. TRIO now commands widespread bipartisan support, but it did not in the summer of 1995.

I blocked this rescissions package for two weeks. I did not agree to time limits on amendments, which meant I was prepared to talk and talk and use every delaying tactic I could think of. When I first started this filibuster, I was joined by Senator Carol Moseley-Braun. She spoke eloquently about the hardships these cuts would impose on low-income communities and people of color.

Senator Dole was anxious to recess for the August break, but our delay made that impossible. He became increasingly frustrated and angry and condemned our tactics. One evening, Sheila and I were watching C-SPAN in our apartment with her father. Senator Dole was out on the floor expressing his frustration with me for my obstructiveness and lack of comity. He was definitely not pleased. Sheila's dad turned to me and said, "What is he going to do with you?" I replied, "Nothing. He'll get over it." Indeed, I always appreciated the way Robert Dole could disagree or even be furious with you one day and then be perfectly civil the next day. He was a skillful legislator who loved the process.

Dole agreed that we had to compromise, and we saved some important government funding that helped people. Most important, this fight set a positive tone for Democrats in the Congress and communicated an important message to the White House. Robert Novak—no liberal!—wrote a column pointing out that even though it was the ultraliberal Paul Wellstone using obvious confrontation tactics, other Democrats did not seem to mind. In fact, he said, they seemed supportive. Novak felt Democratic legislators were telling the Democratic administration that they wanted to see some fight. I think Novak was right. For too long, the president was nowhere to be found. It was time for him to exert leadership. Indeed, when the president did come out fighting for Medicare and the environment and middle-class issues, he gained support and rose dramatically in the polls.

One fight I took on that didn't win me many friends was a reform effort called the gift ban. I couldn't believe all the gifts, free meals, trips, and other perks lobbyists and various special interests showered on senators and their staffs. To me this was a serious ethics issue. How could ordinary citizens believe in the integrity of the political process if we were receiving all these gifts?

The first opportunity for reform came when Carl Levin, one of the two or three senators I admire most, brought a lobbying registration bill to the floor. Levin's legislation tightened the loophole-ridden registration rules so the public could know much more about lobbyists' activities and expenditures. My amendment required lobbyists to file reports, twice a year, that included a member-by-member accounting of the benefits, including gifts and meals, bestowed on lawmakers. This would be a huge step forward. The political problem was not with the public and certainly not with Minnesotans, who were all for this kind of change. The problem was with senators who, while they would never publicly vote against the amendment, took it as a personal attack.

I was told, in no uncertain terms, not to introduce this amendment. "It is insulting to imply that we are influenced by being taken to lunch," they said. I could not believe their anger. Fortunately, reform groups like Common Cause and others backed me all the way and reminded me daily of the righteousness of our cause. This was important because I could feel the bipartisan hostility of other senators. At one of the weekly Democratic caucus meetings, I listened to a significant number of colleagues vent their frustrations with lobbying disclosure and gift ban legislation. They accused me of demeaning public service by accusing them of being dishonest.

The lobbying disclosure amendment passed the Senate on a voice vote. Unfortunately, my colleagues killed my amendment in conference committee. For two more years, I persisted, with the help of Russ Feingold, John McCain, Frank Lautenberg, and Carl Levin. We were determined to bring gift ban legislation to the Senate floor for debate and an up-or-down vote. Majority Leader Dole and Republican Whip Lott were equally determined to prevent a vote. I announced, after one year of their stalling, that we intended to tie the Senate up by introducing a gift ban amendment to every piece of legislation that came to the Senate floor.

After we did so on several major bills, Dole and Lott agreed to give us floor time. On July 28, 1995, the Senate passed, by a 98–0 vote, tough new gift rules. These new rules banned "charity" golf and tennis outings that gave senators free vacations. They also imposed a hundred-dollar annual ceiling on gifts from any single source and banned lobbyist contributions to senators' legal-defense funds and "policy retreats." Despite the eventual unanimity, we almost lost. Right before the final vote, Trent Lott introduced a poison-pill amendment that exempted any gift of under fifty dollars from applying to the annual limit. The amendment passed narrowly. (Many senators did not really want to give up their favors.) Mike Epstein, my tactically adept legislative director, had reserved one final amendment slot for me for just this kind of eventuality. We came back with an amendment that pretty much closed the Lott loophole: All gifts valued at more than ten dollars would be counted toward the hundred-dollar limit.

This rule change applied to the Senate and took effect the following January. The House of Representatives felt the pressure and also passed more stringent gift rules. We may have bucked our parties and made some colleagues very angry, but the public wanted this change, so we could not be denied.

I am convinced you have to be tenacious and scrappy to be effective in the Senate, especially in these partisan times. Consider the appointment of judges. I've been lucky enough to recommend Diana Murphy to be the first woman to serve on the Eighth Circuit Court of Appeals and to recommend four great judges (that is, half the court) to the U.S. District Court for Minnesota. All have been confirmed. One of them, Michael Davis, is the first African American ever to serve on that court. These judges will probably be my most enduring contributions to Minnesota and our country. But what battles their nominations took, and what civics lessons they taught about how the Senate really works.

Judge Davis and Judge Donovan Frank sailed through the confirmation process. But Jack Tunheim and Ann Montgomery were different stories. The irony is that in some ways they were more "moderate" than the other two. But confirmation of judicial nominees, a vitally important decision, often has very little to do with their qualifications.

Jack Tunheim and his family were scheduled to come to Washington so that he could appear before the judiciary committee and answer senators' questions. This was to be a very special moment for Jack and his family, as it probably is for all judicial nominees.

But I had been battling Majority Leader Dole on the rescissions bill and had held up the Senate for three weeks. He was furious with me. Dole wrote up a unanimous-consent request. He would request that a list of pending nominees appear before the judiciary committee for confirmation. He sent a copy of the list to the Democratic cloakroom. Jack Tunheim's name was *explicitly* crossed out.

I spent almost the whole day waiting for Dole to come to the floor. I sent a message to the Republican cloakroom: "Please tell the majority leader that I am going to have a picture taken of Jack Tunheim and his wife and children. I am going to release the picture to the media with a statement about how they paid for their airplane tickets and were refused a hearing because of retaliation by the majority leader regarding a completely separate issue. This is not very presidential."

Robert Dole, who clearly was soon to be campaigning for president, reconsidered! Can you believe this is the way decisions get made?

Ann Montgomery did a great job before the Judiciary Committee, but almost a year went by before she was confirmed. Part of the problem was that the Republicans were delaying all Democratic nominations, but there was more to it. After months of pressing for a vote, Trent Lott, who was by that time the majority leader, assured me that Ann would go through. But when the moment came for her to be confirmed along with a number of other judges by a voice vote, there was an objection to her. A single senator can object and put a hold on a nomination. In this case, the senator was Kay Bailey Hutchison. She obviously was angry that I was holding up approval of a nuclear-waste dump site in Sierra Blanca, Texas (as I described earlier), and she clearly intended to use Ann's confirmation as leverage to force me to "go away" on Sierra Blanca. Ann watched this in horror on C-SPAN.

I told Lott the next day that the Senate would "do no business for four days." I intended to block everything. The Senate was scheduled to recess in a few days and Lott wanted to complete more work. I'll never forget what he said to me: "I believe you." That's all he said. I did block all Senate action for the next two days, after which Lott worked something out with Hutchison, and Ann Montgomery was confirmed by the Senate to serve as a federal judge. She told me later that she couldn't believe this process. I don't blame her. The only thing I know is that she was one of the last judges confirmed (in early August) until after the 1996 election.

—

One way you can make a real difference as a senator is by introducing amendments on the floor. For example, I proposed an amendment to the Department of Defense authorization bill requiring medical personnel at military bases to keep reports of domestic violence confidential. Women were afraid to report violence because their husbands and others could immediately find out they had done so—with frightening consequences sometimes.

Here's another example: an amendment to a foreign-operations bill requiring the State Department in its annual country-by-country human rights report to include a separate section on "sex trafficking"—the use of women in prostitution or forced labor. And another: an amendment to ensure that a higher-education bill provided Pell grant assistance to summer-school students, many of whom are older and support children.

I could list many other amendments of this kind. They make a positive difference in people's lives, and it is a great feeling to know your work has a national or even international impact. But these are small victories and a far cry from what I hoped I could accomplish as a senator.

An activist senator can try to attach an amendment to any piece of legislation. Trent Lott may want to talk about tax cuts, but through an amendment a tenacious senator can force debate over child poverty or prescription drug benefits for the elderly. The majority leader, however, in the past two years, has taken steps to prevent this kind of debate. On bill after bill, from tax cuts to trade bills, the majority no longer tolerates even a day's worth of debate before moving "to bring to a close the debate upon the bill," also known as cloture. Sixty votes are required to end debate.

Beyond limiting debate, the majority is using cloture to force the minority into forgoing its right to offer amendments. Majority Leader Lott typically makes a take-it-or-leave-it offer: Either muzzle your right to amendments or you will be painted as an obstructionist; either get our approval in advance for your amendments or have no amendments at all.

If cloture is invoked, Lott wins the day. The legislation passes with few, if any, amendments attached. If all forty-five Democrats are united, then the cloture vote is not successful and Senator Lott withdraws the legislation. If you are trying to prevent debate and votes on tough issues such as minimum wage, patient protection, prescription drug coverage, or campaign finance reform, this is an ideal strategy, especially if you are not in favor of active government policy in the first place. No tough votes and no new government programs.

Most of the time, Democrats are united. But sometimes, when at least some Democrats favor a bill, or when they are afraid to look like they have blocked legislation, a senator's right to introduce and debate amendments goes by the wayside, to the detriment of the institution.

When George Mitchell and Robert Dole were majority leaders, we would plow through amendments. There might be sixty or even ninety amendments to a bill, and it would take us a solid week, from early morning to late night, to get the work done. But this was the Senate fulfilling its historical mission: We debated, we voted, and we passed or defeated legislation.

Majority Leader Lott has now made the Senate a place where it is harder to be a good or great legislator. In trying to run it like the House of Representatives, his actions have drained some of the vitality and uniqueness of the Senate. It is extremely important that when Democrats regain the majority, we do not do the same. Every time I enter the chamber of the Senate, I get goose bumps. It is a place steeped in history, filled with the desks of luminaries such as Daniel Webster, Robert La Follette, Wayne Morse, Robert Taft, Hubert Humphrey, and Robert Kennedy. My desk (not in the same company as these great statesmen!) is next to Ted Kennedy's. Kennedy occupies his brother John's desk. The drawers of these desks still bear their former occupants' names, etched in the wood.

The Senate is one of the few places in government where all points of view can be heard. Every senator can make his or her case. It is completely different from the House of Representatives, where members have to seek permission from a leadership-dominated rules committee to offer an amendment. In the House, minority rights hardly exist.

Since bills have to pass both the House and the Senate, conference committees can become obstacles to even small victories. I can understand how and why Congress won't pass universal health care coverage or "right to organize" labor-law-reform legislation. I know the realities of power and the ideological debate. What I cannot understand or accept are the decisions made in conference committee. Over and over again, I will pass amendments in the Senate that are then taken out by a conference committee. Some legislators use this mechanism to make it look as if they are for something initially, and then they take it out in conference committee, where it is almost impossible to know how or if members voted.

Here's an example: I pass an amendment to a bill that authorizes support programs at the community level for children who witness violence in their homes. The House Republican majority, probably with the acquiescence of Republican senators, strikes this provision from the bill. "Why the opposition to this?" I ask myself. "How could they do this? What is the objection to providing some help to these children?" Over and over again, I find myself asking these questions, with more and more indignation.

Paul Simon often reminded me not to get personal. These Republicans don't think this is the federal government's role. One time in the Committee on Health, Education, Labor, and Pensions (HELP), we were debating this exact amendment. Tim Hutchinson from Arkansas argued against it, citing all the existing federal programs for children. His position was that we didn't need yet more government programs. I vehemently disagreed with him. "Tim," I asked, "aren't we here to help people? I've identified a crucial need. These children need help. That is why we are here, to pass legislation that will help and improve the lives of people." Ours are two very different philosophies of government. I do appreciate Tim Hutchinson, and, a million disagreements notwithstanding, we are friends.

But part of my anger is with the process. The current majority also diminished the Senate by changing in 1996 the rule that limits what can be incorporated into a conference report. If the majority chooses not to work with the minority in conference committee, which is now the norm, the members of the majority can meet in private, add or subtract whatever provisions they like, and send the bill to the floor. Provisions passed by both the House and Senate can be taken out, and provisions passed by neither body and com-

pletely unrelated to the scope or subject matter of the original legislation can be included. The majority can roll over the minority.
This is not about whose ox is being gored. It is about the dignity
of the U.S. Senate. An amendment to restore the rule with regard to
conference reports was defeated 51–47, in a nearly party-line vote.
When Democrats regain the majority, we must restore this rule.
Otherwise, the Senate will lose its crucial capacity to represent minority rights.

A case study I'll use in class when I go back to teaching is the
"bankruptcy reform" bill. On November 4, 1999, the Senate began
floor consideration of the Bankruptcy Reform Act, the House having passed a similar measure (which had 106 cosponsors) six
months previously by a margin of 313 to 108. Ultimately, the Senate would pass the bill on February 2, 2000, with eighty-three yea
votes. This overwhelming bipartisan support, along with millions
of dollars in lobbying fees paid by the financial-services industry
and millions more in campaign contributions poured into both parties, would seem to make this legislation a slam dunk for the bill's
backers.

The credit card industry argued that there was widespread abuse
of the existing bankruptcy law. Too many irresponsible people were
unwilling to pay back their loans, they said. Charles Grassley (now
chair of the powerful Finance Committee) was the chief author of
the bill on the floor. He is, in my opinion, one of the most effective
senators: He is experienced, has great staff to back him up, and is
very popular. Grassley, whom I thoroughly enjoy as a friend, absolutely believed in this legislation.

But the bill imposed harsh penalties on families who file for bankruptcy in good faith as a last resort, rewarded predatory and reckless lending by banks and credit card companies, and did nothing to actually prevent bankruptcies by promoting economic security. The vast majority of bankruptcies were caused by major medical bills, loss of job, or divorce. Current bankruptcy law was a major safety net for the middle class in America. People could file Chapter 7, pay off what debt they could, but not lose everything. They could rebuild their lives.

I could not believe Democrats voted for this legislation. A less harsh bankruptcy bill had passed the Senate a year earlier on a 99–1 vote. (I voted against it.) This legislation was far worse: It would financially destroy families who had to file bankruptcy through no fault of their own.

One amendment adopted by the Senate gave me one chance, however slim, to stop this bill. Senator Domenici offered an alternative amendment to a minimum wage amendment by Senator Kennedy. Domenici's amendment reduced the wage amount and provided $30 billion in tax cuts for small businesses. The Constitution directs that all measures that raise revenue must originate in the House of Representatives. As there were no tax provisions in the House-passed bill, and to protect its constitutional prerogative, the House would insist that the tax provisions be stripped out before the bill could be sent over for a conference. But it would take unanimous consent in the Senate to strip out the offending amendment, meaning that any one senator could block the bankruptcy bill from moving forward.

On March 22, Lott asked unanimous consent on the floor of the Senate to split the Domenici minimum wage/tax cut from the Senate bankruptcy bill and to go to conference with the House on bankruptcy. I objected. This was an opportunity for a minority of one to block further consideration of a bad bill.

Month after month, I objected. Luckily, time was on our side. We built some grassroots presence—consumer, labor, civil rights—against the bill. The bill was a good target. One secretly included provision gave lenders the right to require that, as a condition of granting a loan, the borrower exercise his right to waive protection of his pension. Naturally, such a waiver would be buried in the fine print of a loan agreement; only a pension lawyer would understand what the borrower was giving up. I lashed out at the industry for this "pension grab." A group of us—Kennedy, Harkin, Boxer, Schumer, Feingold, and Durbin—held press conferences, joined by consumer organizations, blasting the bill. The pension grab provision was dropped.

Time magazine's May 15 cover story was titled "Soaked by Congress." It was a detailed exposé of the bankruptcy bill and the millions of dollars behind it, written by Pulitzer-winning reporters Bartlett and Steele. I circulated the article to all ninety-nine of my colleagues.

The White House now joined the fight with hints that the president might be willing to veto the legislation if it were not more balanced. Over the next several months, there was a steady drumbeat of critical stories and editorials on the bill routinely referred to as "controversial bankruptcy legislation." For the first time, momentum seemed to shift to our side.

Majority Leader Lott, as the months dragged on, was determined. He announced, "Until the last breath that's taken in the 106th Congress, we will be looking for a way to get bankruptcy to the president." There were rumors he would attach the bill to a conference report on crop insurance or a conference report on violence against women and sex trafficking. Minnesota is an agricultural state, and I had helped write the other legislation. So how could I, and for that matter the rest of the Senate, oppose these conference reports? Fortunately, Lott didn't do this, I believe, because it was too transparent and looked too cynical.

Finally, on October 12, with Congress already one week past its target adjournment date for the year, the bill's proponents showed their hand when the House voted to go to conference on a State Department authorization bill that the Senate had requested a conference on in August 1999. The text of that State Department legislation had been included in an omnibus measure at the end of 1999, so the substance of the authorization bill was moot. At the beginning of October, I had started getting commitments from the leadership before I agreed to unanimous consent requests to go to conference on other bills that bankruptcy provisions not be included. But the Senate had already requested a conference on this bill, making this a perfect vehicle. Two hours after voting to go to conference, the Republican conferees agreed to strip out all the language related to the State Department bill, insert the text of a new bankruptcy bill in its place, and file the conference report in the House. The next day, the House passed the conference report by voice vote.

I immediately announced my intention to block the conference report once it got to the Senate. Realistically, however, because a conference report is considered "privileged business" in the Senate, my options were limited. Still, I could at least drag the fight out over a few days. On October 19, White House chief of staff John

Podesta sent a letter to Lott and Speaker Hastert indicating that the White House would veto the conference report.

A veto of the bill now seemed very likely—even a pocket veto if Congress adjourned within ten days of sending the bill to the president. But as budget negotiations started to implode, Congress's final adjournment was pushed back further and further. The longer a final vote on the conference report could be delayed, the better the chances were of the president being able to veto the bill with no risk of an override vote. Ironically, Lott also wanted bankruptcy to be the final vote of the session and was waiting to file cloture on the conference report until he could time the cloture vote for the final day of the session. In the meantime, we began trying to sway undecided colleagues.

Finally, on October 30, the week before the election, Lott filed cloture. Unfortunately, a lame-duck session now seemed virtually assured—offering the bill's supporters an attempt to override the president's veto. In addition, the outcome of the election would likely have an impact on the outstanding issues considered in the lame-duck session—perhaps even casting a veto in doubt. It was critical, at a minimum, if cloture was adopted, to try to push the final passage vote on bankruptcy back to after the election. But perhaps there was a chance that cloture could be defeated. It seemed an almost impossible scenario, given the bill's prior support and the fact that Daschle indicated he would support cloture. On the other hand, there were likely to be substantial absentees among Republicans due to the upcoming election. Indeed, only seventy-one senators had been present for Monday's session. Lott needed sixty votes.

On Tuesday afternoon, Dick Durbin and I decided that we would try to defeat the motion to invoke cloture, which would be voted on on Wednesday morning. We asked the interest groups and the White House to make calls. We estimated that there were eighteen Democrats who were likely to vote no on cloture and seven who were virtually certain to vote yes, with the Republicans. We estimated that Lott needed about fourteen Democrats to vote with him, since there were likely to be about eight Republicans absent. Defeating cloture was a long shot.

On November 1, the motion to invoke cloture was defeated on a vote of fifty-three yeas to thirty nays. Lott changed his vote to nay so that he could offer a motion to reconsider the vote at another time. Twenty-nine Democrats voted no, due in large part to aggressive lobbying in the well by myself, Kennedy, Feingold, Boxer, Schumer, and Durbin. As predicted, absentees were critical. The bill's proponents were totally unprepared for this vote. It was a stunning defeat for them.

But this fight was not over. Congress was back in a lame-duck session in December. Lott filed cloture on the bill again and this time broke the filibuster. Seventy-one senators voted for the final passage. It would take thirty-four senators to sustain the president's veto. We were several votes short.

Gene Sperling, the president's economic adviser, felt very strongly about the flaws of this legislation. After we won the cloture vote on November 1, he called me and said, "The little guys won. This hardly ever happens in Washington." Gene assured me the president would veto the bill, that he would not back down. Gene was also very worried that perhaps his boss's last veto in office would be overridden by Congress.

Time ran out for the bill's supporters. The 106th Congress adjourned. There was no way Lott could keep us in session any longer. People wanted to go home! President Clinton could wait ten days and then veto the bill. Congress was not in session to override. The day we left, Chuck Grassley confronted me one more time on bankruptcy—he always did so with humor and grace. "Paul," he said, "can you tell President Clinton to send the bill over to us now, so we can have a chance to override his veto? It would be the right thing for him to do." I said, "Sure, Chuck, I'll call him right away!" He laughed and then told me, "You know, it is amazing—one senator could hold up this bill for almost two years. I have to hand it to you." But it wasn't one senator: It was a coalition of senators and organizations that won this David versus Goliath fight (at least until the Bush administration weighs in). But it felt especially good that a senator with whom I rarely agree but whom I like paid me this compliment.

This is a case study of "playing defense" on bills one opposes. Over the last several years, I feel as if 80 percent of my work as a senator has been playing defense, curbing the extremist enthusiasms of the conservative Republican agenda (much of which originates in the House) rather than moving forward on a progressive agenda. Sometimes, however, there is the opportunity to introduce and pass major legislation that truly helps people. The Trafficking Victims Protection Act, which passed on October 11, 2000, along with the Violence Against Women Act, which passed by a 95–0 vote, are two examples of such legislation.

Enactment of the trafficking-victims legislation, with the help of many people and organizations, is one of my proudest accomplishments. The legislation is a major human rights victory. It will provide funds through USAID to developing countries for public information and election campaigns to *prevent* women from being exploited, and it will require tough persecution of traffickers—including life sentences for trafficking children for forced prostitution. Women would be granted temporary three-year visas so they are not deported when they report abuses, and treatment would be available for women and children who have suffered from abuse.

This is one of the darkest aspects of the new global economy, the trafficking of up to two million women and children—five hundred thousand to the United States—for forced prostitution and forced labor. This legislation will also require the State Department to list those governments that do not cooperate and are complicit in this barbaric practice.

The story of a woman named Rosa illustrates the need for this legislation. When Rosa was fourteen, a man came to her house in Veracruz, Mexico, and asked her if she was interested in making money as a housekeeper in the United States. At the time, she was cleaning rooms at a local hotel and taking care of her little brothers and sisters. She was told that she would make more money as a housekeeper in the United States and that she would be well taken care of. Her parents were worried and told her not to go, but she persuaded them that she should seize this great opportunity. After she decided to leave her town and men smuggled her from Mexico to Orlando, Florida, they told her that she would be forced into prostitution.

Before a hearing I held in the Foreign Relations Committee, she testified,

It was then when the men told me my employment would consist of having sex with men for money. I had never had sex before, and I had never imagined selling my body. And so my nightmare began.

Because I was a virgin, the men decided to initiate me by raping me again and again, to teach me how to have sex. Over the next three months, I was taken to a different trailer every fifteen days. Every night I had to sleep in the same bed in which I had been forced to service customers all day. I couldn't do anything to stop it. I wasn't allowed to go outside without a guard. Many of the bosses had guns. I was constantly afraid. One of the bosses carried me off to a hotel one night, where he raped me. I could do nothing to stop him. Because I was so young, I was always in demand with the customers. It was awful. Although the men were supposed to wear condoms, some didn't, so eventually I became pregnant and was forced to have an abortion. They sent me back to the brothel almost immediately. I cannot forget what has happened. I can't put it behind me. I find it nearly impossible to trust people. I still feel shame. I was a decent girl in Mexico. I used to go to church with my family. I only wish none of this ever happened.

Between February 1996 and March 1998, Rosa and from twenty-five to forty other Mexican girls and women were trafficked from Veracruz to Florida and the Carolinas. The girls had been promised jobs as nannies, housekeepers, and as home health attendants for the elderly. They were subjected to forced prostitution, rape, assault, and forced abortions. In March 1998, sixteen men were arrested and indicted in Florida state court. After trial, they received sentences ranging from two and a half to six and a half years.

In 1996, a prostitution ring involving women trafficked from the Ukraine and Russia was broken in Bethesda, Maryland. The women had answered ads to be au pairs, sales clerks, and waitresses but were forced to provide sexual services and live twenty-four hours a day in a massage parlor across from the Bethesda public library. The women had been assaulted repeatedly and were deeply traumatized. When the case went to trial, the Russian-American massage-parlor owner was fined. He entered a plea bargain, and the charges were dropped with the restriction that he could not operate a business again in Montgomery County. The women, who had not been paid any salary and had been charged $150 for their housing, were deported.

This case was a dramatic example in the Senate's own backyard of the breathtakingly light penalties that traffickers received in these cases (more clearly understood as slavery cases). The sentences did not reflect the multitude of human rights abuses perpetrated against the female victims.

The stories of women and children like Rosa, exploited by traffickers, were so compelling that they gave rise to an unusual coalition of conservative religious groups, feminist organizations, and human rights groups to pass trafficking legislation. William Bennett and Gloria Steinem joined hands in this effort. And I reached out to Sam Brownback, a socially conservative senator from Kansas. We were a most unusual coalition, joined by Chris Smith and Sam Gejdenson (another broad coalition) in the House.

It took three years to pass this legislation. The challenge was to get this coalition to agree on every point. A very contentious question was whether Congress should focus on sex trafficking alone and not on labor trafficking. Then there was the White House and the State Department. Undersecretary for Human Rights Harold Koh was especially concerned about sanctions. He strongly believed that automatic sanctions against governments would be counterproductive. Some organizations in our coalition felt just the opposite. Finally, various senators wanted to claim jurisdiction over the legislation and write different provisions. It took years to negotiate all these disagreements and reach a compromise. It took literally hundreds of hours of staff time.

I cannot say enough about Sam Brownback. He enlisted the support of Majority Leader Lott at the same time I was constantly battling Lott on the floor on other issues. Sam felt strongly about this exploitation and made this legislation his priority. Remember, this was not a constituency that could contribute big bucks. Interestingly enough, Jesse Helms felt just as strongly and weighed in for us. Never in my wildest imagination did I think I'd be working with these guys!

There was one final hurdle. We needed unanimous consent to pass the conference report with limited debate. Otherwise, the majority leader would pull the bill from the floor. There was very little time left in the session, and he needed the floor open for other legislation.

We heard no objections from Senate offices and were ready to briefly speak and vote on the bill when I spotted Tom Harkin and John McCain on the floor and saw big trouble ahead.

First I spoke with Harkin. He said, "I am not going to let any bill move until there is a vote on the floor to confirm Bonnie Campbell to the U.S. Court of Appeals. They have blocked her nomination, and I am going to fight." Tom is my best friend in the Senate, so I could appeal to him to please first let this legislation, which I had been working on for three years, pass. He agreed.

I then hustled over to McCain. He was all set to "get the floor" and bring the Senate to a halt. McCain, like Harkin, was livid. He had been blocked by Lott from a vote on a reform bill (not campaign finance reform) and had decided to object to any unanimous-consent agreement. "Paul," he said, "I have no choice, I am going to shut the Senate down. I'm sorry." I pleaded with him to let us quickly pass this human rights bill. He looked at me hard. I'm convinced he budged only as a favor to a friend. Personal relationships can be so critical in the Senate. If Tom Harkin and John McCain had not helped a friend, the trafficking legislation would not have passed. I never had a feel for this when I was teaching about the ten steps a bill goes through in Congress.

Quite often, it's important as a senator to take on vested power. I think this is where the Democratic Party is weakest. On large questions dealing with power in America, on "class issues," most Democrats are nowhere to be found. When it comes to funding for Head Start, affordable child care, more investments in job training, housing, health, and education, the differences between Democrats and Republicans make a difference. But not when it comes to challenging economic power in America. The same powerful investors control both parties. I hate saying this—it is the most discouraging thing about being a senator—but it is a reality.

International trade agreements without any enforceable child-labor, fair-labor, human rights, or environmental standards pass with overwhelming majorities that include many Democrats. "Financial modernization" legislation, written specifically for the giant financial institutions, passed with eighty-eight votes! My amendment calling for a moratorium on mergers and acquisitions of large agricultural conglomerates got only twenty-nine votes. Many senators tell me, "I am sympathetic, but I have to satisfy my agribusiness back home." They dare not challenge the dominant economic interests in their states. Indeed, they justify their votes by equating these interests with their states' interests. In many decisive sectors of our economy, we are seeing a frightening concentration of power—telecommunications, health insurance, agriculture, banking, and energy, to name a few major examples. Yet the Democrats have little to say. Too many in the Senate Democratic caucus are no more willing to challenge "the heavy hitters," "the players," "the well-connected," and "the investors" than are the Senate Republicans.

It is one thing to know the Senate rules and to fight hard for what you believe in. That doesn't mean, however, that you are able to pass important legislation that can dramatically improve people's lives. In October 1999, the *Congressional Quarterly* listed the "fifty most effective members of Congress." I was proud to be included. But their summary gave me pause: "Wellstone earns this distinction under the banner of 'liberal stalwart,' along with Democratic Representatives John Lewis of Georgia, Barney Frank of Massachusetts and Charles Rangel of New York. . . . Wellstone is less a legislator than a liberal voice of conscience."

How does being a "liberal voice of conscience" help people I love and care about who need help *now*? Being a "voice of conscience" doesn't help farmers who are losing their businesses and families;

senior citizens who cannot afford prescription drugs; the mentally ill who have no treatment; poor and hungry children; students receiving inadequate educations; people without health care coverage; children who have given up; people who lack affordable housing; workers in low-wage and dangerous jobs; those who suffer domestic violence; children who witness violence at home and need help; people who need substance-abuse treatment; or those condemned to snake-pit "juvenile justice" facilities. Time is not neutral for them. It is so hard to see what needs to be done, to hear the pleas for help, and to realize you can't bring about the necessary change. I never thought I would feel powerless as a U.S. senator. Most of the time I don't, but I sometimes struggle with what to say to them.

During one of my regular school visits, I had a memorable experience at P.S. 30, an elementary school in the Mott Haven community in the South Bronx. I met Aida Rosa, the sixty-three-year-old principal, whose family wants her to retire. She won't. She will never give up on these children. Nor will Martha Overall, the Episcopalian vicar at the Church of St. Ann. Or many of the unbelievable teachers that Aida Rosa has attracted. Yet few of the students there will ever graduate from high school. Can't we do something about this before it's too late?

I came back to the Senate the next day and introduced an amendment to the $290 billion Pentagon budget that would transfer $1 billion of it, a relatively small amount, to the Title I education program, providing more help—reading help, after-school care, and prekindergarten programs—for low-income children. I was thinking of these children and writer Jonathan Kozol, who has had such a big impact on me, as I spoke:

Provide a little more help for poor children in our country not because if you help them when they are young, they are less likely to drop out of school and wind up in prison, though that is true. Not because they are more likely to graduate and to do better in their lives, though that too is true. Not because a little more help when they are young will help them do better in school and contribute more to our economy, though that is true. Vote for this amendment, help them because most of them are less than four feet tall, they are all beautiful, and we should be nice to them.

Fifteen senators voted for this amendment. Senators do not like to vote against a defense budget and be attacked for being weak on national security. And I suppose they were thinking about military contracts in their states. But what about the kids? What about priorities? Just a few years ago, at least thirty to forty senators would have voted to transfer funding from defense to education. We have gone a long way backward. And votes like these leave me only more determined.

I do not want to tell people that everything is rotten in Washington and nothing is going to change. I don't want to tell people, "I agree with you, but I don't have the votes." I don't want to tell people, "We have to get the Republicans out of power before anything good will happen." It just discourages citizen involvement. It is disempowering. It makes people feel powerless.

On the other hand, I cannot promise to pass legislation to change things for the better, because I know that the current political alignment in Washington makes this very difficult. I can promise to fight hard for people, to introduce model legislation to point the way, to be a strong voice for justice. If that is what is meant by being "a liberal voice of conscience," I proudly accept that label. But it is not enough. For me to be truly effective, I have to use my position to organize and galvanize people. Short of a presidential campaign, how do you do so?

The only thing that can beat money politics is a revitalized citizen politics. We need a Senate more broadly representative of people and more responsive to ordinary citizens, who must make their voices heard. There are so many ways for citizens to have a major impact, and the most effective methods of making that impact are the topic of the next chapter.

Chapter 9

—

A WINNING

PROGRESSIVE POLITICS

A progressive politics is a winning politics, as long as it is not organized in a way that is top-down and elitist. It must respect the capacity of ordinary citizens and focus on workaday majority issues.

I have never understood arguments for the need for politicians to "move to the center" to get elected. What is the operational definition of "the center"? If what is meant is that you need to have more votes than your opponent, then I am all for being in the center. But this is too obvious.

If what is meant by the center is the dominant mood of the populace—the issues that are important issues to Americans and what they hope for—then I would again argue for the need to occupy the center. A politics that is not sensitive to the concerns and circumstances of people's lives, a politics that does not speak to and include people, is an intellectually arrogant politics that deserves to fail.

So what is the center? The empirical evidence is irrefutable. Seventy-five percent of voters think business has too much influence in Washington. Seventy-one percent agree that companies that lobby and give political contributions while getting government contracts are taking part in "legalized bribery." About three quarters of voters believe that at least half the time members of Congress make decisions based on what their contributors want.

Fifty-four percent of voters agree that the "economic boom has not reached people like [them]." Sixty-one percent believe that the projected budget surplus should be invested either in education and public schools or in expanded health care coverage. Just 18 percent prefer an across-the-board tax cut. By a two-to-one margin, American voters believe that free trade costs more U.S. jobs than it creates. Fifty-three percent oppose permanent normalization of trade with China. A majority (52 percent) believes that there should be tougher regulations to "restrain corporations from moving jobs overseas, polluting the environment and treating workers badly."

When I am in coffee shops with people (these are great focus groups), no one asks, "Are you left, right, or center?" No one cares. What people want is that your politics be about them. Tip O'Neill once declared, "All politics is local." But I would go further; all politics is personal:

"Senator, I am seventy-five years old. My monthly income is six hundred dollars and my prescription drug costs are three hundred dollars. I can't afford it. What can I do?"

"Senator, our daughter was anorexic. She was a beautiful girl. She was down to eighty pounds but the insurance plan would still not approve hospital costs."

"Senator, I just lost my job. I worked for the company for thirty years. Now I am fifty-six and have no health care coverage."

"Senator, I direct a battered women's shelter. Every thirteen seconds, a woman is battered in her own home. But though she and her children must leave to be safe, we don't have enough beds and shelters for them. We have twice as many animal shelters in our country."

"Senator, my wife and I both work. Our combined income is thirty-five thousand. We have two small children, two and four, and child care costs us twelve thousand a year. Is there any help for us?"

"Senator, I am a child care worker. I love working with small children. But I make, with a college education, nine dollars an hour, and I don't have any health care."

"Senator, I am fifty years old. Should I hold on to our farm and burn up all my equity, or get out now? Will we get decent prices again? Do I have any future?"

"Senator, my wife and I both work long hours. We have no choice if we are to make a living. But we hardly ever have time for our kids. It is rare that we even get to have dinner as a family together."

"Senator, my parents are in their mid-seventies and declining health. I try to help them. But is there more help so they can continue to stay at home and not be put in a nursing home? They will lose everything if they are put in a home."

"Senator, I love teaching these kids. We are a good inner-city elementary school. We really are committed to the children. But these children come to school hungry. How can they learn?"

"Senator, we don't have the counseling or mental health services to help kids who are struggling in our rural community."

"Senator, please get some substance-abuse treatment for this Vietnam veteran. Without help, he will stay homeless and in bad shape."

"Senator, both political parties are controlled by the same big interests. They don't care about us."

If you ask people at the Town Talk Café in Willmar, Minnesota, how many of them consider themselves liberals and how many conservatives, the response is about 25 percent to 75 percent. But if you get beyond the labels and probe a little further, you'll find that the overwhelming majority can't stand the pharmaceutical companies, oil companies, insurance companies, grain companies, and packers. They don't like big anything—big government or big corporations. But they want the government to be on their side and would agree with Teddy Roosevelt that "government must make sure that the power of wealth is used for and not against the interests of the people as a whole." They believe that government today too often serves the interests of the already powerful and wealthy.

I think the 1994 elections were all about this populism, as was the election of Jesse Ventura as governor of Minnesota in 1998.

I should have been able to predict the Gingrich victory in 1994. It was staring me in the face one night in Wabasha, Minnesota, in mid-February. About one hundred people crammed into the bowling alley for a town meeting. The overwhelming sentiment expressed to me in no uncertain terms was, "Senator Wellstone, give us access to some capital, and get the government out of our way.

We are self-sufficient, self-reliant people." Small-business owners emphasized that for them the government was far more a problem than a help. There was too much unreasonable regulation and not enough reasonable help.

I was in agreement with what I heard—a powerful critique of overly centralized and overly bureaucratic government policy. As a former community organizer who spent most of my time trying to empower poor people to make decisions for themselves, I believed in their model of economics. It is far better that the men and women who own businesses live in the community, that the business be locally owned rather than buffeted by crucial decisions made over martinis halfway across the country or around the world. The people in Wabasha didn't say it this way, but they understood this. They wanted a homegrown economy. They believed in local entrepreneurship, in self-reliance and self-sufficient communities.

This sentiment, in a different way, was expressed across the country in November 1994. This was a downright antiestablishment, anti–status quo, "throw the rascals out" election. Democrats were then in the majority, so it was a logical conclusion to throw them out. Indeed, Newt Gingrich, in a stroke of genius, nationalized the elections by spreading a message of empowerment to citizens. The election, however, begged the question of what kind of change people voted for. Speaker Gingrich was mistaken that Americans supported his harsh agenda.

In 1998, Jesse Ventura, a former professional wrestler, ran for governor of Minnesota as a third-party candidate and, in his words, "shocked the world" by defeating Democrat Skip Humphrey, the son of Hubert H. Humphrey, and Republican Norm Coleman, the mayor of St. Paul. These two experienced and very capable politicians didn't see it coming. I didn't either, until the last two weeks. He was figuratively giving the finger to politics as usual. His campaign was populist and brilliant. He was Minnesotans' revenge against a politics that they perceived as fake and phony and dominated by money interests. Minnesotans felt like both parties had it coming to them, and Ventura, with 37 percent of the vote, won the election.

The people of Minnesota clearly expressed their anger toward politics, an anger that many Americans share. That does not mean that people do not care what happens. They care deeply, sometimes desperately. But they also feel that their own struggles, the cares of their daily lives, are of little concern in the chambers of power, that whomever they choose will make little difference to them, their loved ones, and their communities.

This is not a conservative America. These are people who more than anything else yearn for a politics they can believe in. They want politicians whom they can trust and who are at least most of the time on their side.

Their voices are not statistics, their fears and hopes are not measured by a consumer price index or gross national product. According to the averages and indicators, this is a prosperous time for our country. It is a time of substantial growth and low inflation, of a booming stock market and low unemployment. But averages are misleading. They tell nothing of the ends of the curve—the height at the top or the depth at the bottom.

The averages say nothing about the people I have met in my travels and described in this book. They say nothing about the children in Tunica, Mississippi, or the students in Louisiana studying desperately to pass a high-stakes test. The statistics tell nothing of the *millions* of Americans who don't have health insurance and live in terror of getting sick.

If I had to use labels, I would say that public opinion is populist and "center-left" on the issues. Yet politics, especially national politics, is "center-right." Why the contradiction? The highly respected pollster Celinda Lake has data that are very instructive. Voters and donors (the top Democratic and Republican contributors) have widely divergent views on crucial reform and economic issues when given a specific example. Lockheed spent eight million on lobbying and contributions this past year and received thirteen billion dollars from the federal government. Donors are evenly split over whether this amounts to a bribe or is the normal way of doing business; *voters*, however, by a 71 percent majority, look at this as legalized bribery. Even more important are the starkly different economic views held by donors and voters. The greatest number of donors (40 percent) think everyone has benefited from the economy, while 64 percent of voters think the wealthy or big corporations have benefited the most. The donors' top policy choice is tax cuts; the majority are against tougher environmental and workplace regulations; and by a two-to-one margin they believe free-trade policy creates more jobs in the United States than it costs. The voters have, by the same margins, the exact opposite view. This same divide exists over normalizing trade relations with China.

This polling data on the disconnect between big givers and voters tells an important story about American politics. The financial imperative severely weakens the policy performance of both parties. The investors dominate the rank-and-file party voters.

The gap is even greater, I believe, between the donors' political viewpoint and that of the American populace at large, not just voters'. There is, of course, a 50 percent hole in the electorate in presidential elections, and this hole is stratified by class. Nonvoters are disproportionately low-income, blue-collar, people of color, and young. They come from a different world than the donors and put a much higher priority on bread-and-butter economic issues. Their viewpoint matters even less than the ordinary voters' because they don't produce votes and are not threats to officeholders.

Clearly, there is a forgotten American majority. It is precisely this America that our politics today fails to serve fully and fairly. This America faces major challenges: low wages, insufficient health care, nonexistent pension coverage (the majority of private-sector workers have no pension coverage), daunting child care expenses, rising college expenses, and exorbitant housing costs. These Americans can't hire lobbyists. They can't fly senators and congressmen to resorts. They don't fill the campaign coffers of political candidates. Only when these Americans are given a proportional voice in politics can we claim to live in a truly representative democracy.

The challenge is to make a place for all Americans at the decision-making table, to force our political leaders to listen to their concerns, and for them then to take action. Renewing democracy will not happen overnight or without a very difficult fight. But it is a dream that can be realized. There are three critical ingredients to democratic renewal and progressive change in America: good public policy, grassroots organizing, and electoral politics. Policy provides direction and an agenda for action; grassroots organizing builds a constituency to fight for change; and electoral politics is the main way we contest for power and hold decision makers accountable.

Public policy is not just an academic exercise or a philosophical exercise about hypothetical problems. Public policy affects all of us, where we live and where we work.

Policy is not about techniques of communication. Over and over again I hear my Democratic colleagues talk about how to better deliver our "message." But the question is not how to communicate our agenda, but whether we have an agenda worth communicating. Throughout this book, I have discussed a variety of policy initiatives that I believe speak to the real concerns and circumstances of people's lives.

People yearn for a politics that speaks to and includes them. They are not getting that today. Instead, we have what the eminent political scientist Walter Dean Burnham calls "the politics of excluded alternatives." Jim Hightower calls it a "downsized politics." Despite record economic performance, both political parties still tell us that the federal government cannot afford to help working families in our country. This kind of politics leaves out a majority of the people.

At least Republicans are consistent. They argue that when it comes to these pressing issues of people's lives, there is very little the government can or should do. But most people don't accept this. Most people know that this is a great philosophy only if you are wealthy.

One student at the University of Michigan said to me, "Senator, I want to be able to dream again—about a better country and a better world. And politics today doesn't give me a chance to dream."

There is a huge leadership void in this country that the Democratic Party, emboldened by political courage and a commitment to the issues that made our party great, can fill. Self-interest is more than economic self-interest; it is also how you feel about yourself. Are you living a life consistent with the words you speak, are you helping others, are you helping your community or your country or your world? A winning politics is a politics of values that appeals to the best in people, that enables citizens to dream again to make a better America. Bobby Kennedy was right: We can do better.

Too many progressives make the mistake of believing people are galvanized around ten-point programs. They are not! People respond according to their sense of right and wrong. They respond to a leadership of values.

Not only do Democrats have too timid and downsized an agenda, we also have failed to confront conservatives on core value questions. I call the Republicans' philosophy the "New Isolationism." Not as in foreign affairs, but in human affairs. It is a "Buddy, you're on your own" philosophy. If you are losing your family farm, if you can't afford prescription drugs, if you have no health insurance, if you are working forty hours a week but are still poor and unable to support your children, if you are a homeless Vietnam veteran struggling with mental problems, you're on your own.

Whatever happened to "There but for the grace of God go I"? Or "Love thy neighbor as thyself"? We need to replace isolationism with fellowship. We need to talk about community, about justice, about the goodness of America. People are ready for a politics that inspires them to be their best. Stephen Carter, in his book *Civility,* describes how, in the early days of the railroad, people who were crowded together on an arduous journey cooperated and were good to one another, out of common necessity. We as a country need to realize that we are on a common journey and that we all need to give a little and help one another so we can all get to where we want to go.

But it is not enough to inspire people with vision and good public policy. We need the power to make the change. Effective grassroots organizing is the way to get there. Grassroots organizing involves listening to and lobbying and advocating for people by going directly to where they live and work. It is the antithesis of big-money politics. Organizing at the grassroots requires hard and mostly unglamorous work, easily identifiable goals, and political sophistication. But it can be enormously effective and successful.

The good news is that there is some great organizing taking place in the country. Under John Sweeney's able leadership, the AFL-CIO is committed to "organizing the unorganized." It is a different labor organization—no longer just middle-aged white men lobbying in Washington. They are reaching out to women and people of color, building coalitions in neighborhoods and communities.

The Service Employees International Union is also leading the way. President Andy Stern insists that 50 percent of the union's budget goes to organizing. The results are dramatic: SEIU successfully organized seventy thousand home health care workers in Los Angeles. I spent some time visiting these workers during the organizing drive. They were mainly Latinas who earned little more than six dollars an hour, with no health care benefits. In very personal terms, they told me (in Spanish) about their elderly and disabled patients. They were very proud of helping people. I had to probe to get them to focus on the working conditions, which were deplorable. Now, a year later, they belong to a union and they make more than ten dollars an hour, with full health care benefits. Now their work will be valued. This is what the organizing of the unorganized is all about.

Throughout the labor movement, energy has replaced the old complacency. When Democrats controlled the Congress for so many years, labor relied on interest-group politics. If there was a problem, you called the committee or subcommittee, where you had a long-standing relationship. The grassroots base withered away while the "Christian right" learned how to mobilize support. They became good at our forgotten game: voter registration, door knocking, phoning, electing people to school boards, writing letters to the editor, calling in to talk radio, turning out voters. Now labor and other progressive organizations must learn from their example.

Right after I was first elected to the Senate, the AFL-CIO organized a "labor solidarity" march in Washington. Only a few members of Congress joined in because we weren't in session at the date chosen. I remember thinking, "Why bring workers to Washington when Congress is in recess? They need to feel the heat." But this huge march wasn't connected to any fight. Representatives and senators, out of town, felt no pressure.

At the end of the march, I suggested a follow-up to the AFL-CIO leaders. What about a "labor solidarity" day in individual states? After all, Washington, D.C., was too long or expensive a trip for many members, and we could organize some tough face-to-face accountability sessions with representatives and senators in their home districts. We could do it all across the country. I might as well have been talking to a man on the moon.

Contrast this attitude with labor's march in the other Washington, what became known as the "battle in Seattle." It was only eight years later, but these were light-years for organized labor. Unions focused on organizing *and* on rank-and-file member education. They had learned another lesson. Mailings sent out to members with a list of union-endorsed candidates didn't cut it. It was time to focus on issues and education and empower members, armed with information, to make choices.

It was organized labor and the organized environmental community that brought forty thousand people to Seattle to challenge the World Trade Organization. They were joined by family farmers, representatives of allied nongovernmental organizations, members of the human rights community, and students. It was amazing to hear steelworkers and Teamsters emphasize the environment at their rallies, and to hear environmental leaders speak at these labor rallies! Steelworkers and environmentalists are a potent coalition. The gathering in Seattle should be viewed with a sense of history. Good organizing recognizes how institutional changes affect people and create organizing possibilities, and this work at the end of November 1999 may prove to be a milestone in this regard.

One hundred years earlier, as the U.S. economy began to shift from local units to national interests, the country saw wrenching economic times. Labor conditions were exploitative. Family farmers were driven off their lands. These conditions gave rise to the populist and progressive movements, with a daring set of what at that time seemed like impossible demands: the right to organize, a forty-hour workweek, the right of women to vote, direct election of U.S. senators, action against trusts. The political system was even more dominated by big money than it is now. Labor organizers were murdered. The media were hostile. Yet these demands, an effort to civilize an emerging national economy, eventually became the basis of new laws.

The demands in Seattle, made by a populist, progressive coalition led by labor and environmentalists, are aimed at civilizing an emerging global economy—to make a global economy work not just for multinational corporations but also for working people, family farmers, the environment, and human rights. Whether this coalition will hold is the question. But one thing is certain: Trade policy can never be discussed again without questions concerning child labor, the right to organize, the environment, and human rights. The potential exists for new and exciting progressive coalitions. The adage "Think globally and act locally" is being replaced with a new wisdom: Act locally and act globally.

It is also heartening to see the success of "living wage" campaigns across our country, which demand that governments require businesses with whom they do business to pay a decent wage to their employees. It is an important, new definition of employment: not just a job but a job paying a reasonable wage with reasonable benefits as well.

The progressive religious community is also finally finding its voice. People are building inner city/inner suburb coalitions again, around economic issues: jobs, housing, transportation to get to the jobs, health care, and education for children. What is so exciting about this organizing is the emergence of new coalitions. Never before have these citizens seen their common interests and organized together to fight for their children and communities.

Public Campaign is also embracing a grassroots approach to reform. This is completely different from interest-group lobbying in Washington. The premise (with which I agree) is that comprehensive campaign finance reform cannot be won in Washington, especially when the system is wired for incumbents who are not that anxious to change the laws. Rather, a citizen politics has a much better chance of defeating a money politics at the state level, where progressives can form grassroots organizations.

"Clean money, clean elections" victories in Maine, Vermont, Massachusetts, and Arizona point the way—those states now have voluntary public financing of state elections. I saw with my own eyes the fascinating energy and coalition of citizens behind these successful initiatives. In many living rooms, people who had never known one another, and indeed in the past may have opposed each other, came together to fight successfully for authentic democracy.

These victories will provide models for and provoke the hopes and aspirations of citizens in other states. The only cautionary note I would sound about this organizing concerns the danger of "dead-end localism." Victories should be won by people where they live, but if the victories never affect national or international centers of decision-making power, then we are still not seriously contesting for power. This is the central challenge for progressive politics: how to build the local victories into a strong national and international presence that can crucially define the quality of life. Right now the whole does not equal the sum of the parts. Amazing people have done so much to make their communities better, but progressives hold little power on the national level.

Electoral politics is one crucial way we contest for power in America, and progressives need to get better at it. We tend to be attracted to politics because of the issues and far less excited by the nuts-and-bolts mechanics of political campaigns, much less the compromises that are inevitable in those campaigns.

I've met hundreds of great young organizers but very few young people who are campaign managers on any level. Electoral politics seems unsavory—and indeed it can be, depending on who is involved. The problem is that progressives fail to build leadership and gain power when we eschew electoral politics. You can be certain that the "Christian right" develops local leadership and runs candidates for school boards. Progressives too often don't. In every state, we need to get serious about developing leaders—starting with school board, city council, county commissioner, mayoral, and state legislative races. Money is much less a factor in these races than it is nationally, and well-organized citizen campaigns can win over and over again.

I am shocked at how little of this work is being done, at how few progressives there are who have the interest and the skills to manage political campaigns. We have to figure out a way to engage many more people in electoral politics. If we build our progressive political leadership, state by state, then we will also be in a much stronger position to thrust forward candidates for governor and for seats in the House of Representatives and the Senate. Right now, it is the same-old same-old approach in the Democratic Party. I thought it was bad in 1990 when I first ran for Senate, but it has gotten even worse. The DSCC is focused almost totally on whether a candidate is wealthy, already has power and status, or has access to big bucks. These criteria are not likely to produce many progressives focused on populist and economic-justice issues. A few might slip through, but they will be exceptions.

It can be an alienating experience to attend a Democratic Party luncheon focused on upcoming Senate races. Too much of the time is spent on fund-raising, and when I hear the DSCC report on candidates, it is the usual conventional wisdom about who can win and why, and who can't.

Bernard "B" Rappaport, a very wealthy contributor to the Democratic Party and Democratic candidates, was recently honored at a DSCC dinner. Different senators spoke in glowing terms about B, and then it was his turn. He started out by saying, "I am scared to death. I'm wondering what all this is going to cost me." There was a good-humored, not cynical, laugh by all in the room. He then spoke for one more minute (usually B is quite a talker). He said, "I know all of you, and you are all good people. But I know that often you don't vote what you really believe in. I am eighty years old, and my wish is for the Democratic Party to get back to principles and to really stand for something."

This is my wish as well. But it is not going to happen on present course. We need to build not a third party but an independent political force that does a lot of organizing within the Democratic Party—especially candidate recruitment and elections. This new political force must introduce fresh perspectives into the political dialogue of our country; recruit candidates; provide the training, skills, and resources for winning campaigns; build an infrastructure of field directors and campaign managers; have a savvy media presence; apply effective grassroots organizing to electoral politics; and build political leadership at the local, state, and federal levels of government.

There is a wave of social activism on our campuses today, more than I've seen in the past fifteen years. But most of these students are not joining the Young Democrats. I went to a very poignant neighborhood meeting in Minneapolis, with more than one hundred people crammed into a home. Almost all of the people there were under thirty. Most were professionals. Their exclusive focus was on issues: education, health care, housing, the environment, and community service. They had little interest in politics as usually defined—candidates, political parties, and elections. They were incredibly bright and thoughtful, but as it stands they will not be future political leaders. Which is why politics as usual shouldn't work any longer. An independent progressive politics, combining intellectual integrity, grassroots organizing, and electoral politics, is a force whose time has come.

I intend to work with progressives around the country to make this happen. Always, with a twinkle in my eye, I will represent the Democratic wing of the Democratic Party.

But regardless of what I decide to do in the future, I will remain actively engaged and committed to the issues and causes outlined here. I have dedicated my life to the cause of economic justice and equality of opportunity for all Americans.

The famous abolitionist Wendell Phillips was once asked, "Wendell, why are you so on fire?"

He responded, "I'm on fire because I have mountains of ice before me to melt."

So do we.

ACKNOWLEDGMENTS

Thanks to Bill Dauster and Kelly Ross for their ideas and help with the book. Bill Lofy put this work, with many good suggestions, in electronic form, since my brain still goes to a pen and many yellow tablets. Jonathan Karp, despite his many sharp comments (such as "We get the point!"), is a great editor and made this book better. David Black was the one who gave me the encouragement to write this book. Elly Zaragoza and Connie Lewis always made sure I had the time to write—even if it was from 5:00 A.M. to 7:00 A.M. They are two wonderful and supportive colleagues. Colin McGinnis, my chief of staff, *always* makes sure that the work gets done!

A B O U T   T H E   A U T H O R

PAUL WELLSTONE grew up in Arlington, Virginia, and attended the University of North Carolina at Chapel Hill, where he earned his B.A. and Ph.D. in political science. He was a professor of political science at Carleton College in Northfield, Minnesota, for twenty-one years before being elected to the United States Senate in 1990. He and his wife, Sheila, have three children and six grandchildren.

ABOUT THE TYPE

This book was set in FF Celeste, a digital font that its designer, Chris Burke, classifies as a modern humanistic typeface. Celeste was influenced by Bodoni and Waldman, but the strokeweight contrast is less pronounced, making it more suitable for current digital typesetting and offset-printing techniques. The serifs tend to the triangular, and the italics harmonize well with the roman in tone and width. It is a robust and readable text face that is less stark and modular than many of the modern fonts and has many of the friendlier old-face features.